The
Surrender
Experiment

The Surrender Experiment

my journey into life's perfection

Michael A. Singer

HARMONY

BOOKS · NEW YORK

Copyright © 2015 by Michael A. Singer
All rights reserved.
Published in the United States by Harmony Books, an imprint of the Crown
Publishing Group, a division of Penguin Random House LLC, New York.
www.crownpublishing.com

Harmony Books is a registered trademark, and the Circle colophon
is a trademark of Penguin Random House LLC.

The Surrender Experiment™ is a trademark of Shanti Publications, Inc.

Library of Congress Cataloging-in-Publication Data is available upon request.

ISBN 978-0-8041-4110-9
eBook ISBN 978-0-8041-4111-6

Printed in the United States of America

Book design by Amanda Dewey
Jacket design by Fort & Jess Morphew
Jacket illustration by Shutterstock/David M. Schrader

26 28 30 29 27

First Edition

To the Masters

Contents

Section IX

Total Surrender   *215*

Acknowledgments

In truth, life is really the author of this book. She is the one who manifested the flow of events that were so powerful and fascinating they demanded narration. But life needed me to put pen to paper if her greatness was to be memorialized. To that end, she sent exactly the right people at exactly the right time to bring *The Surrender Experiment* into fruition.

It is with humility and heartfelt thanks that I tell you of the phenomenal job that my product manager, Karen Entner, did on this book. Her tireless and selfless service has instilled this work with a sense of commitment and perfection rarely found in this world.

I would also like to take this opportunity to thank my editor, Gary Jansen, from Crown Publishing, for all the hard work and great suggestions he contributed. As would be expected, life provided the absolutely perfect editor to assist me in giving this testimony to her greatness.

This book had many early readers, all of whom deserve thanks. I would like to single out James O'Dea, Ursula Harlos, and Stephanie Davis, who contributed detailed suggestions on draft after draft during the early stages of writing.

I now get to acknowledge you, the reader, for having the interest and taking the time to read about this phenomenal experiment. May we all learn to appreciate our lives in this amazing universe—a little bit more each day.

The
Surrender
Experiment

Section I

Waking Up

The Premise

Sitting alone in a six-seater private jet at forty thousand feet is a very peaceful place. I fell into meditation and my mind became very still. When I opened my eyes, I absorbed the tremendous difference in my environment from when I had first moved out to the woods to be alone and meditate. Though I still lived in those same woods, my place of solitude had grown into a thriving yoga community, and I had become CEO of the public corporation that life had somehow magically manifested around me. It was now perfectly clear to me that all of these life experiences, including running a business at this level, were doing as much to free me spiritually as my years of solitary meditation. Just as Hercules used the flow of rivers to clean out the Augean stables, so the powerful flow of life was cleaning out whatever was left of me. I just kept letting go and practicing nonresistance, whether I liked what was happening or not. It was in this frame of mind that I was flying off to Texas to discuss the billion-dollar merger offer for my company from a powerful CEO whom I had never even met.

My Reflections, May 1999

L ife rarely unfolds exactly as we want it to. And if we stop and think about it, that makes perfect sense. The scope of life is universal, and the fact that we are not actually in control of life's events should be self-evident. The universe has been around for

13.8 billion years, and the processes that determine the flow of life around us did not begin when we were born, nor will they end when we die. What manifests in front of us at any given moment is actually something truly extraordinary—it is the end result of all the forces that have been interacting together for billions of years. We are not responsible for even the tiniest fraction of what is manifesting around us. Nonetheless, we walk around constantly trying to control and determine what will happen in our lives. No wonder there's so much tension, anxiety, and fear. Each of us actually believes that things should be the way we want them, instead of being the natural result of all the forces of creation.

Every day, we give precedence to our mind's thoughts over the reality unfolding before us. We regularly say things like, "It better not rain today because I'm going camping" or "I better get that raise because I really need the money." Notice that these bold claims about what should and shouldn't be happening are not based on scientific evidence; they're based solely on personal preferences made up in our minds. Without realizing it, we do this with everything in our lives— it's as though we actually believe that the world around us is supposed to manifest in accordance to our own likes and dislikes. If it doesn't, surely something is very wrong. This is an extremely difficult way to live, and it is the reason we feel that we are always struggling with life.

Nonetheless, it is also true that we are not powerless in the face of the events unfolding around us. We have been gifted with the power of will. From deep inside, we can determine how we want something to be and apply the power of our minds, hearts, and bodies in an attempt to make the outside world conform. But this puts us in a constant battle of our way versus the way it would be without our intervention. This battle between individual will and the reality of life unfolding around us ends up consuming our lives. When we win the battle, we are happy and relaxed; when we don't, we are disturbed and stressed. Since most of us only feel good when things are going our way, we are constantly attempting to control everything in our lives.

The question is, does it have to be this way? There is so much evidence that life does quite well on its own. The planets stay in orbit, tiny seeds grow into giant trees, weather patterns have kept forests across the globe watered for millions of years, and a single fertilized cell grows into a beautiful baby. We are not doing any of these things as conscious acts of will; they are all being done by the incomprehensible perfection of life itself. All these amazing events, and countless more, are being carried out by forces of life that have been around for billions of years—the very same forces of life that we are consciously pitting our will against on a daily basis. If the natural unfolding of the process of life can create and take care of the entire universe, is it really reasonable for us to assume that nothing good will happen unless we force it to? It is to the exploration of this intriguing question that this book is devoted.

How can there possibly be a more important question? If life can manifest the DNA molecule on its own, not to mention create the human brain, how is it that we feel that we have to control everything on our own? There must be another, more sane way to approach life. For example, what would happen if we respected the flow of life and used our free will to participate in what's unfolding, instead of fighting it? What would be the quality of the life that unfolds? Would it just be random events with no order or meaning, or would the same perfection of order and meaning that manifests in the rest of the universe manifest in the everyday life around us?

What we have here is the basis for an amazing experiment. At the heart of the experiment is a simple question: Am I better off making up an alternate reality in my mind and then fighting with reality to make it be my way, or am I better off letting go of what I want and serving the same forces of reality that managed to create the entire perfection of the universe around me? This experiment would not be about dropping out of life; it would be about leaping into life to live in a place where we are no longer controlled by our personal fears and desires. For lack of a better name, I have called this "the surrender experiment," and to the best of my ability, I have devoted the last forty years of my life to seeing where the flow of life's events would naturally take me. What happened over the course of these four decades is nothing short of phenomenal. Not only did things not fall apart, quite the opposite happened. As one thing naturally followed the other, the flow of life's events led me on a journey that would have been beyond my comprehension. This book shares that journey with you so that you can experience what happened when someone dared to let go and trust the flow of life.

Let it be clear right from the start, however, that this type of surrender does not mean living life without the assertion of will. My story of these forty years is simply the story of what happened when the assertion of will was guided by what life was doing instead of what I wanted it to be doing. My personal experience is that aligning one's will with the natural forces unfolding around us leads to some surprisingly powerful results.

The only effective way to share the results of this great experiment is to allow you to see how I got pulled into living this way and then allow you to experience the journey as I did. In what follows, you are about to encounter a set of life experiences that are bound to be very different from your own. I share these with you only because as human beings we have the extraordinary ability to learn from one another's experiences. You don't have to live as I did in order to be affected by what happened to me. The unexpected events that unfolded before me not only changed my life, they changed my entire view of life and left me with a sense of deep inner peace. Hopefully, sharing my surrender experiment with you will encourage you to find a more peaceful and harmonious way to live your life and to better appreciate the amazing perfection that unfolds around us.

1.

Not with a Shout—But with a Whisper

My given name is Michael Alan Singer. From as far back as I can remember, everyone has called me Mickey. I was born May 6, 1947, and lived a fairly ordinary life until the winter of 1970. Then something happened to me that was so profound that it forever changed the direction of my life.

Life-changing events can be very dramatic and, by their very nature, disruptive. Your whole being is headed in one direction physically, emotionally, and mentally; and that direction has all the momentum of your past and all the dreams of your future. Then suddenly, there's a major earthquake, a terrible sickness, or a chance encounter that totally sweeps you off your feet. If the event is powerful enough to change the focus of your heart and mind, the rest of your life will change in due course. You are literally not the same person on both sides of a truly life-changing event. Your interests change, your goals change, in fact, the underlying purpose of your life changes. It usually takes a very powerful event to turn your head around so far that you never look back.

But not always.

In the winter of 1970, no such event happened to me. What happened was so subtle, so faint, that it could easily have passed by without being noticed. It was not with a shout but with a whisper that my life was thrown into utter turmoil and transformation. It has been more than forty years now since that life-changing moment, but I remember it as if it were yesterday.

I was sitting on the living room couch in my home in Gainesville, Florida. I was twenty-two years old and married at the time to a beautiful soul named Shelly. We were both students at the University of Florida where I was doing my graduate work in economics. I was a very astute student, and I was being groomed by the chairman of the economics department to become a college professor. Shelly had a brother, Ronnie, who was a very successful attorney in Chicago. Ronnie and I became close friends even though we were from totally different worlds. He was a powerful, wealth-driven, big-city attorney, and I was a '60s-groomed, college-intellectual hippie. It is worth mentioning just how analytically oriented I was at the time. I had never even taken a philosophy, psychology, or religion course while in college. My electives at school were symbolic logic, advanced calculus, and theoretical statistics. This makes what happened to me all the more amazing.

Ronnie would come down once in a while to visit, and we would often just hang out together. As it turns out, Ronnie was sitting on that couch with me on that fateful day in 1970. I don't remember exactly what we were talking about, but there had been a lull in our leisurely conversation. I noticed I was uncomfortable with the silence and found myself thinking of what to say next. I had been in similar situations many times before, but something was quite different about this experience. Instead of simply being uncomfortable and trying to find something to say, I *noticed* that I was uncomfortable and trying to find something to say. For the first time in my life, my mind and emotions were something I was watching instead of being.

I know that it is difficult to put into words, but there was a complete sense of separation between my anxious mind, which was spewing out possible topics to talk about, and me, the one who was simply aware that my mind was doing this. It was like I was suddenly able to remain above my mind and quietly watch the thoughts being created. Believe it or not, that subtle shift in my seat of awareness became a tornado that rearranged my entire life.

For a few moments, I just sat there inwardly watching myself try to "fix" the awkward silence. But I was not the one trying to fix it; I was the one quietly watching the activity of my mind trying to fix it. At first there were only a few degrees of separation between me and what I was watching. But every second the separation seemed to become greater and greater. I was not doing anything to cause this shift. I was just there noticing that my sense of *me* no longer included the neurotic thought patterns that were passing in front of me.

This entire process of "becoming aware" was practically instantaneous. It was like when you stare at one of those posters that has a hidden picture inside. At first it appears to be just a circle with line patterns. Then, suddenly, you see an entire 3-D image emerge from what originally looked like chaos. Once you see it, you can't imagine how you hadn't seen it before. It was right there! Such was the shift that happened inside of me. It was so obvious—I was in there watching my thoughts and emotions. I had always been in there watching, but I had been too unaware to notice. It was as though I had been so involved in their details that I never saw them as just thoughts and emotions.

Within seconds, what previously seemed like important solutions for how to break the uncomfortable silence was now sounding like a neurotic voice talking inside my head. I watched as that voice tried out things to say:

The weather's been awesome, hasn't it?
Did you hear what Nixon did the other day?
Do you want to get something to eat?

When I finally did open my mouth to say something, what I said was:

"Have you ever noticed that there's this voice talking inside your head?"

Ronnie looked at me a little weird, and then a spark lit in his eyes. He said, "Yes, I see what you're talking about—mine never shuts up!" I distinctly remember making a joke out of it by asking him what it would be like if he heard someone else's voice talking in there. We laughed, and life went on.

But not *my* life. My life didn't just "go on." In my life, nothing would ever be the same again. I didn't have to try to maintain this awareness. It was who I was now. I was the being who was watching the incessant flow of thoughts pass through the mind. From the same seat of awareness, I watched the ever-shifting current of emotions pass through the heart. When I showered, I saw what that voice had to say while I was supposed to be washing my body. If I was talking to someone, I watched as that voice figured out what to say next—instead of listening to what the other person was saying. If I went to class, I watched my mind play the game of trying to think ahead of the professor to see if it could figure out where he was going with the lecture. Needless to say, it did not take long before this newly found voice inside my head really started to annoy me. It was like sitting next to someone in a movie theater who never, ever stops talking.

As I observed that voice, something deep inside my being just wanted it to shut up. What would it be like if it stopped? I began to long for silence inside. Within days of that first experience, my life's patterns began to change. When friends came over to socialize, I no longer enjoyed the scene. I wanted to quiet my mind, and social activities didn't help. I began to excuse myself and go out to the woods near our house. I would sit down on the ground amid the trees and tell that voice to shut up. Of course, it didn't work. Nothing seemed to work. I found that I could change the topic it talked about, but I could not get it to just stop talking for any length of time. My yearning for inner silence became a passion. I knew what it was like to watch the voice. What I didn't know is what it would be like if the voice totally stopped. And what I never could have imagined was the life-changing journey on which I was about to embark.

2.

Getting to Know Me

Even in my youth, I loved to figure out how things worked. So it was inevitable that my analytical mind would become fascinated by trying to understand my relationship to the voice inside my head. Before I could enjoy this intellectual fascination, however, I had to get over the fact that the personal mind was driving me crazy. Every time I saw something, that voice made some comment about it: *I like it . . .; I don't like it . . .; I'm not comfortable with this . . .; This reminds me of . . .* As I became more and more accustomed to watching all this, a few questions naturally arose. First, why is this voice talking all the time? If I see something, I'm instantly aware of seeing it. Why does the voice have to tell me that I see it and how I feel about it?

Here comes Mary. I don't feel like seeing her today. I hope she doesn't see me.

I know what I see and I know what I feel. After all, I'm the one in here seeing and feeling. Why does it have to get vocalized in my mind?

Another question that arose was who am I who keeps noticing all this mental activity? Who am I who can just watch thoughts come up with a complete sense of detachment?

I now had two driving forces awaken inside regarding this newly found voice in my head. One was the desire to shut it up and the other was the pure fascination and yearning to understand what that voice was and where it came from.

I mentioned that prior to this inner awakening, my life was pretty ordinary. I only say that in comparison to what my life became. I became a driven human being. I wanted to know about the voice I had discovered, and I wanted to know who I was—the one inside experiencing all of this. I began to spend hours on end in the graduate school library. But I was not in the economics section; I was in the psychology section. There was no way that others had not noticed this voice talking inside. It was so prevalent that you couldn't miss it. I scanned through Freud trying to find the answers to my questions. I read book after book, but I found no direct reference to the voice talking inside—not to mention any reference to the one who is aware that the voice is talking.

In those days, I would talk about the voice to anyone who would listen. They all must have thought I was crazy. I remember one encounter with my very reserved, highly cultured Spanish professor. I ran into him one day between classes and excitedly told him that I had come to understand what it meant to be fluent in a language. I explained to him that there was this voice inside your head that talks to you about virtually everything—what you like and dislike, what you're supposed to be doing right now, and what you've done wrong in the past. If that inner voice could speak in Spanish and you immediately understood what it was saying, then you were fluent in Spanish. If, however, the Spanish words made no sense to you until you did the mental work of translating them so that the voice would repeat them in English, then you were not fluent in Spanish. It made perfect sense—to me. I told him that if I were majoring in language studies, I would do my doctoral dissertation on that premise. Needless to say, my Spanish professor gave me a very odd look, said something very polite, and went on his way.

I didn't care what he thought. I was on an exploration, a journey of learning beyond anything I could have imagined. Every day I was learning so much about myself. I couldn't believe the amount of self-consciousness and fear being expressed through that voice. It was so obvious that the person I was watching inside cared a great deal about what people thought of him. This was especially true of people I knew well. The voice told me what to say and what not to say. It complained incessantly when something was not the way it wanted. If a conversation with a friend ended with the slightest discord or disagreement, the conversation would keep going on inside my head. I would watch the voice wishfully imagine how the conversation could have ended on a different note. I could see how much fear of rejection and nonacceptance were being expressed through that mental dialogue. It was overwhelming at times, but I never lost the perspective of watching a voice talking inside. It was obvious it wasn't me; it was something I was watching.

Imagine if you woke up one day and a cacophony of noise was all around you. You wanted it to stop, but you had no idea how to stop it. That is the effect the voice was having on me. One thing was perfectly clear: that voice had always talked before. But I had been so lost in it that I never noticed it as separate from me. It was like a fish not knowing it is in water until it gets out. One leap into the air and the fish instantly realizes, "There's a body of water down there, and that is where I've always been. But now I see that I can get out."

I didn't like the voice of the mind talking all the time. It was just like an irritating noise that I really wanted to stop. But it didn't. For now I was stuck with it. As it turns out, however, I had not yet begun to fight.

3.

The Pillars of Zen

Months went by and I was still on my own with my inner exploration. Little did I know that help was about to arrive unexpectedly.

I had a classmate in my doctoral program named Mark Waldman. He was a bright young man and an avid reader on a broad range of subjects. Like everyone else, Mark had heard me talking about my interest in the voice. One day he brought me a book he thought might help. The book was entitled *Three Pillars of Zen,* by Philip Kapleau.

I knew absolutely nothing about Zen Buddhism. I was an intellectual who didn't give religious matters a second thought. I was brought up Jewish, but not very much so. By the time I reached college, religion played no part in my life. If you had asked me if I was an atheist, I probably would have given you a blank stare. I had never even thought about it.

I started leafing through the pages of the book on Zen, and within minutes it became evident: this book was about that voice. My heart practically stopped. I had trouble breathing. This book was clearly about how to stop that voice from talking. Passage after passage spoke about quieting the mind. It used terms like the *True Self* behind the mind. There was no doubt that I had found what I'd been looking for. I knew there had to be others who had gained the perspective of watching that voice of the mind instead of identifying with it. Not only was there an entire legacy of knowledge spanning thousands of years that dealt with the voice, but this book clearly discussed "getting out."

It talked about freeing yourself from the hold of the mind. It talked about going *beyond*.

Needless to say, I was in awe. I felt a reverence for this book that I had never felt for anything in my life. I had been forced to read and study so many books in school. I now had in my hands a book that answered some real questions for me, like who am I that watches that voice talk. These were questions that I passionately wanted to know the answers to. Truth is, it was way beyond *want*. I *needed* to know these answers—that voice was driving me crazy!

What *Three Pillars of Zen* had to say was very clear and unequivocal. It said to stop reading, talking, and thinking about your mind, and just do the work necessary to quiet it down. The required work was equally unambiguous—meditate.

Before I even knew about meditation, I had tried sitting alone in order to make the voice stop talking. But that had never worked for me. With this book, I was presented a tried-and-true method that had worked for thousands of others. Simply sit down in a quiet spot, watch your breath go in and out, and mentally repeat the sound *Mu*. That's it. Now do that for an ever-increasing length of time each day. In Zen, the real work was generally done in a group setting called a *sessin*. In traditional settings, a trained person would walk around with a *kyosaku* stick. If you started to sleep or lost focus in another manner, you would get a smack on your shoulders with the stick. Zen was strict; there was no playing around. This form of Zen was serious work.

I didn't have a group or a teacher. All I had was the book and a very sincere yearning to see if these practices would take me where I wanted to go. So I started to do Zen meditation on my own. At least it was my best understanding of what Zen meditation is. At first I sat for fifteen or twenty minutes each day. Within a week I built that to half an hour, twice a day. There were no fireworks or deep experiences. But concentrating on my breath and the mantra was definitely diverting my awareness from the incessant chatter of the voice. If I made the mental voice say *Mu*, it couldn't say all the crazy personal things it usually said. I quickly began to like the practice. I looked forward to the times I had put aside during the day for meditation.

I was no more than a few weeks into my experiment with Zen meditation when Shelly and I decided to go on a camping trip. We were joined by four friends, and together we drove our vans into Ocala National Forest for the weekend. I had a VW camper, so weekend trips were an easy affair. But this trip wouldn't turn out to be just another camping trip—this trip was destined to have a profound impact on the rest of my life.

We found a secluded spot in the woods that opened up to a pristine wetland area. Once we situated our vans, we were overcome by the quiet and beauty of the place. It dawned on me that this would be a good place to do some meditation. I was just a novice, but I was very serious about doing the practices and finding out what it would be like if the voice actually stopped. I asked Shelly and our friends if I could spend some time by myself. No one objected, so I meandered down by the grassy lake and found a nice spot to sit. The whole notion of meditating was so meaningful to me that from the start it was like a sacred experience. I picked a tree to sit under, just like the Buddha. Then, very dramatically, I told myself, *I'm not getting up until I've reached enlightenment.*

What happened under that tree that day was so powerful that even now my body shivers and my eyes begin to tear just to think about it.

4.

Absolute Silence

I crossed my legs in a full-lotus position. I knew I wasn't proficient enough to hold that posture for long, but I thought I might as well start with the official meditation position. I straightened my back and neck, and I began to concentrate on my breath expanding and contracting in my abdomen. The Zen book instructed me to make the *Mu* sound way down in my belly, below the belly button. I watched my breath go in and out from way down there.

I was intending to sit for much longer than I had done previously, so I used my will to concentrate with extra intensity and sincerity. It must have made a difference because I went deeper inside than I had ever gone before. It seemed that concentrating on the movement of the breath in my belly created a force that linked the outflow of breath from my nostrils with the inner movement of my abdomen. Every time I breathed slowly out my nose, I felt a warm, inviting sensation throughout the area below my belly. The sensation was so nice that my attention naturally centered there. For a period of time, I simply lost myself in the beauty of the experience.

Some time later, the length of which I had no way of telling, the mental voice began talking about how beautiful the experience was and how this must be real meditation. Since my awareness was drawn to that mental voice, it was drawn away from concentrating on the breath. The meditation experience seemed to have run its natural course, and I began to come down to my normal mental state.

But this meditation session was supposed to be different. I had told myself I wasn't getting up until I had broken through. So I willfully began concentrating anew on the movement of the breath in my belly and on the sound of *Mu*. I lost myself once again in the warm flowing force that tied my exhalations to the warmth in my abdomen. The force became much stronger as I concentrated more deeply. Eventually, all consciousness of my body and my surroundings was gone. I was only aware of the effortless flow of warm energy that was building and expanding at the core of my belly. I was not there; only the flow was there.

From time to time, for brief moments, my sense of self-awareness would drift back into focus. The instant that started to happen, I would willfully focus on the feeling of the exhaled breath and the movement of my belly—and, instantly, I was no longer there. This experience of drifting in and out of the deep state went on for a prolonged period of time, perhaps hours.

At some point, I must have lost the will to refocus during one of those moments when self-awareness returned. I had been far gone in a very deep and peaceful place, but I started to come back. I don't know how long I had actually been sitting, but the first thing I became aware of was the pain in my legs. They hurt a great deal from sitting in a full-lotus position for so long. The voice of the mind had not started back up yet. I was just there, kind of dazed, but very peaceful and deeply mesmerized by the experience. I suppose I would have continued to come down, but an amazing thing happened. From back behind where my sense of awareness had been centering came a booming voice. It said very sternly: "DO YOU OR DO YOU NOT WANT TO KNOW WHAT IS BEYOND YOU?"

This was not the voice of the mind I was so used to struggling with. Ever since I first noticed that chattering voice, it was talking in front of and below where I sat inside. This new invocation came from behind and above where my sense of awareness was now situated. In any event, its stern challenge shook me to the depths of my being. I didn't feel the need to answer the question, because every drop of me yearned to go deeper. So I took a breath in, then deeply pushed myself into the out-breath, and I was gone.

When my sense of self-awareness began to coagulate again, my experience of being was very different from anything I had ever experienced before. I felt pain in my legs, but they were very far away and the pain had a warmth and beauty to it. As I regained some awareness of my body, I tried to lean my head a tiny bit forward. Nothing moved. It was as though my forehead was pressed against a wall. Something very solid was resisting even the slightest movement of my head forward. I immediately realized that the sheer intensity of my concentration had created a well-defined force that flowed outward from my forehead and curved back to the point in my lower abdomen where I had been concentrating. I know this must sound strange, but it felt like a magnetic field that was so strong I simply could not move against it.

This was not the only powerful energy I was experiencing. I had been sitting in a full-lotus posture with my hands resting on my crossed feet. In that position the whole of my hands, arms, and shoulders formed a closed circle. Now that complete circle had become another one of these force fields. I could neither move forward nor sideways—I was locked in what I can only describe as perpendicular energy flows. Whenever I breathed out, the flows became more tangible and intense. The entire experience was so completely enthralling that I did not actually regain awareness of my surroundings. I only came down far enough to see that my body was overcome by these energy flows. Then, once again, I heard: "DO YOU OR DO YOU NOT WANT TO KNOW WHAT IS BEYOND YOU?"

I immediately took a deep breath in and with great intention slowly exhaled through my nostrils. It was as though the outgoing breath pushing against the magnetic force fields created upward lift. That upward and inward propulsion began to drive me to an even deeper place, beyond any sense of self-awareness. One more breath in and out, and I was completely gone.

Perhaps you would like to ask where I went. That's reasonable, but I'm unable to answer that question. I only know that each time I came back, I was in a more elevated state than when I left. When I came back from nowhere the next time, everything was very different.

There was no subtle resistance to having returned. There was no sense of urgency to hold on to the elevated state. There was only peace—deep, deep peace. And there was absolute silence, a silence that nothing could possibly disturb. It was so still that perhaps there had never ever been any sound here for all eternity. It was like outer space where there is no atmosphere, so there can be no sound. Sound requires a medium in which to travel. In the place I returned to, there was no such medium. I was truly experiencing the sound of silence.

Most important, there was no voice. There was not even the memory of what it would be like to have chatter in that sacred place. It was gone. All gone. All that was left was awareness of being. I simply existed, nothing more. This time no stern beckoning entreated me to go beyond. It was time to come back.

The first thing I noticed as I became aware of my surroundings was that the external energy flows I experienced earlier had drawn inward. I now felt a very beautiful flow of energy up my spine to the middle of my forehead. I had never experienced this before, and almost all my awareness was drawn to that point. Meanwhile, there was still great pain in my legs, but that wasn't a problem. It was just the quiet experience of pain. No complaints, no mental dialogue about what to do about it. There was simply awareness, completely at peace with what it was aware of.

I managed to move my arms enough to unfold my legs from the lotus position. They were like dead weight, so I lay on my side for a while until they came back to life. It was so peaceful, so comfortable lying there. In time, I opened my eyes. What eased in through those openings was like nothing I had ever seen or dreamed of before. The wetland area before me appeared like a Japanese rice paper painting. It exuded gentleness and stillness. The tall grasses swayed in the gentle breeze, but their movement had a stillness about it. Everything was so quiet, so serene. The trees were quiet, the clouds were quiet, the water was quiet. There was absolute stillness in the midst of the movement of nature. My body was quiet, and there were no thoughts at all.

I could have lain there forever melting into the peace that surrounded my sense of presence.

When I finally got up, the movement of my body was unfamiliar to me. I had never been a graceful person. I was definitely not the dancing type. But now every movement of my body was like a ballet. There was a graceful flow when my arms moved, and I really saw the difference when I began to walk. With each step I could feel every tiny movement of the muscles in my feet. I flowed from one step to the next, and the movement itself was intoxicating.

The amazing part is that this state lasted for weeks. When I rejoined my friends that day, the state didn't change. I felt no need to explain or describe what had happened to me during the two to three hours I was gone. I could hardly talk. Everything was so beautiful and tranquil. The silence, the absolute silence, even sounds outside did not disturb that stillness. The sounds were out there, but they seemed so far away from where I was seated inside. A moat of thick peace allowed nothing to reach the citadel of my elevated state.

5.

From Absolute Peace to
Absolute Turmoil

Shelly and I returned home from the weekend trip, but I could not relate to the life I was coming back to. I had changed completely in a matter of hours. My normal inner state had been transformed into a state of absolute clarity. Neither desire nor fear could touch me in those early days. Even thoughts faded away before reaching my seat of awareness. All I remember experiencing at that time was a powerful, unwavering sense of one pointed intention—*I will never leave this state. No matter what, I will never allow anything to take me from this place.* No voice of my mind had to say that to me; it was who I was. I was no longer Mickey Singer. I was the one who would never betray that peace or allow anything to disturb that transcendent stillness.

I was like a child having to learn everything all over again. I had to learn to eat in a way that was consistent with that peace. I used to smoke pot; I stopped completely. My state was crystal clear, and I didn't want to dull it one iota. I had to learn to go to classes and take tests while remaining perfectly centered. I was in a doctoral program, on full fellowship. I had to learn to use my intellectual mind without disturbing the peace that I now loved more than life itself.

During those next few weeks, I felt like I had been born anew. I found myself yearning to go back beyond. In fact, every time I sat down to meditate I was drawn back into an elevated state. Some veil had been torn aside inside of me, and it was now totally natural to pass back through it. I started waking up at three in the morning to be able to do prolonged meditations. Throughout the day, I would sit whenever and wherever I had the opportunity. Only a small part of my life was about my outer existence. What I was really about was learning to stay deep inside while my outer life passed before me, leaving me at peace.

I wasn't able to stay that detached for long, however. After two to three weeks, the unassailable inner peace began to develop cracks. These cracks allowed the voice of my personal mind to leak back into my sanctuary of silence. I struggled to get it back. Oh, did I struggle. But the struggling itself was inconsistent with the absolute stillness. There was nothing I could do. I had to just sit in here helplessly watching as the Land Beyond My Dreams gave way to my noisy inner state. It never dawned on me that I could try leaving my outer existence in order to maintain the inner stillness. That effort would come a little bit later.

Though my deep inner peace had begun to fade, I never fully returned to my normal state. Even when the personal mind and emotions started back up, I was much further behind them than I used to be. There was also another major change: I was now experiencing a constant flow of energy rising up within me to the point between my eyebrows. It formed a vortex of pressure that forced my attention to that point. For example, if I was looking at something, it felt like I was concentrating my gaze through my brow rather than through my eyes. This didn't affect my ability to see; it just kept me closer to the meditative state at all times. Note that focusing on the energy flow was not something I was doing; it was something that was happening by itself. I was just aware that the flow had never been there before, and now it was always there.

The pull of my attention to the point between my eyebrows became both my teacher and my friend. When my mental voice had something to say, I now had a choice—pay attention to the voice or keep focusing on the inner flow of energy. I eventually realized that if I didn't want to listen to the mental chatter, all I had to do was slightly increase my concentration on the energy flow to my brow. The thoughts would then pass right by without disturbing me. Letting the thoughts go became a game to me. All of life was a lighter experience than before. My personal melodrama would still come up, but it could not pull me down into it. I had been gifted with this inner flow of energy to help me work my way out of myself. More important, I now knew what it would be like to get away from my personal self. My intention was firm and resolute—no matter what it took, or how long it took—I was going to find my way back beyond.

It didn't take long, however, before outer changes began in my life that rivaled the inner changes I was going through. It started with Shelly. One day she told me that it was time to move on. That really threw me for a loop. Though we had only been married a year and a half, the foundation of my personal life had been built around her for years. I tried in vain to hold on to her, but at some point I saw something I had never been able to see before: the sheer strength of my personality and intellect had not given her the room she needed to breathe. If I truly loved her, I had to let her go. Right at that time, I had a friend who needed someone to house-sit while he was away. I moved into that house and began the process of nursing a broken heart.

The sudden change in my outer life had a profound effect on my inner work. I was already totally committed to my regular meditations. Exploring the inner state of deep peace had become the purpose of my life. Now I had another very powerful source of inspiration: I was watching a human being in almost unbearable pain. My heart exuded pain all the time, and my mind was literally broken. It was as though the foundation of my self-concept had been removed, and my personal self was in free fall. I didn't know how to put it together again, nor did I even want to.

If I concentrated very deeply during meditation, all the turmoil melted away. There was silence and peace. The silence was not as thick as it had been before, but it provided me a place of repose. When I came back from meditation, turmoil and pain was what I returned to. So my daily experience was now either heaven or hell. There was nothing in between anymore. My "normal" way of being was gone. In one fell swoop, who I had been—was no more.

More and more I chose meditation. It was not just a way of escaping the pain; meditation gave meaning to my life. I was committed to going beyond—permanently—and the changes in my life were helping me get rid of an entire part of my being that was holding me back. The personality expressing itself through that mental voice was no longer so sure of himself. In fact, he no longer knew which way was up. These outer changes had humbled him. He had thought he had it all figured out—well, he was wrong. It was definitely easier to let go of him when he was in pieces.

During that stage of my growth, I watched very closely as the self-concept attempted to redefine itself. In place of a married man with a defined career path, my thoughts started to envision myself as a meditator who was seeking a deeper truth. But even in those early days I didn't want to regain strength based on another mental concept of myself. Whenever I noticed thoughts being stitched together to create a new "me," I knocked the chair out from under them. It was very painful, but I was willing to let it all go if it freed me to explore beyond.

My friend came back to his house, so I moved out. I didn't care where I lived; I just needed to be alone. My life was pretty simple. I was meditating, doing some yoga, and periodically I would go to class. I had no possessions except my schoolbooks, some clothes, and my VW van. I used to take long drives in the countryside surrounding Gainesville. I had once found a beautiful spot in the woods near a neighboring town where there was a small, abandoned lime pit. The pit was filled with crystal-clear, blue water and was surrounded by nothing but a vast area of scrub oaks and pines. I drove out there, and that is where I lived.

I was becoming more and more of a hermit. It was not so much that I was running away from something—I was running into myself. My intention was very clear at all times: I wanted to go back deep inside myself. My problem was that I had no idea what to do with my personal self—a.k.a. "Mickey." His very existence was holding me back from where I yearned to go. If I didn't work at it, the focus of my attention would keep getting drawn into his personal melodrama. That was clearly the opposite direction from where I wanted to go. "Mickey" was down and out; *I* wanted to go in and up. In those days I was certain of one thing: he was the problem, and he had to go. I had become dead serious about getting rid of him. But I had no idea how.

6.

South of the Border

The summer of 1971 was approaching, and I would soon be free from classes. I was in my second year of graduate school, and though my attendance had not been that regular, I still managed to maintain my high grades. I was studying just enough to do really well on my final exams and written papers. There was no question about what I was going to do with my summer—more meditation and yoga. The only question was, where would I do it?

That was probably the first time in my life that I consciously began to notice a distinct, recurring theme in the events unfolding outside of me. It began when, out of the blue, a classmate asked me if I had ever been down to Mexico. He said it was an interesting place to spend some time. Shortly thereafter, I was in a bookstore and practically tripped over a book about touring Mexico that someone had left on the floor. This started me thinking that maybe I should get away for a while, and maybe Mexico would be a good idea. The final straw was when I went to a gas station to fill up, and someone had left a map of Mexico on top of the pump I was using. Those were enough signs for me. I decided to go off to Mexico.

I didn't know where I was going—Mexico is a pretty big place. But in my state of mind, it really made no difference. I would just go and let it unfold. My friends and family were not all that excited about me going off to Mexico alone with no agenda. I got a lot of warnings about banditos and cautions about avoiding strangers. I spoke some classroom Spanish, just enough to get in trouble. With little more than that, I headed off to Mexico.

My trip took me along the Gulf Coast states and down through Texas. While driving, I would focus on my breath and utter *Mu* in my belly. The last thing in the world I wanted to do was listen to that voice in my head chatter all day. Each night I would find a place to pull over in the woods, meditate, and go to sleep. At that pace, it took a few days to drive down to north-central Mexico, which was where I ended up.

One evening, deep in rural Mexico, I couldn't find any woods to pull into for the night. I didn't feel comfortable just pulling over on the side of the road, so I didn't know what to do. I ended up driving off-road and climbing one of the more gradual foothills until I reached a glorious vista on the crest of a grassy pasture. There were no fences or houses in sight, so that is where I spent the night.

The next morning was breathtaking. A mist floated above the fields, and I could see all the colors of the sunrise. It was so beautiful that I did my morning meditation and yoga postures outside. I went very deep, and an echo of the peace I was seeking overcame my being. I stayed on that grassy hill for many weeks without ever leaving. Each day I increased my periods of meditation and yoga. My mind was quieting down, and my heart was starting to breathe again.

One morning I was startled by a tapping on the side door of my van. I became very scared. Had the banditos finally found me, or was the owner of the land going to throw me off at gunpoint? Upon opening the door, I found a young boy about eight years old standing outside with a container in his hands.

"Esta leche es de mi mama para el Americano en la colina."

I struggled to translate, "This milk is from my mother for the American on the hill." I was so moved, and I thanked him so much. Here I had thought the worst, as usual, and it turned out to be an act of kindness in the middle of nowhere in Mexico.

I was gradually learning that life was not as fragile as that voice in my head would have me believe. There were experiences to be had, but only if you were willing to have them. Most important, that was the first time I can remember crediting life for the flow of events that had unfolded. After all, I hadn't arranged for the perfect place to pull over and spend a few weeks in meditation and solitude, not to mention to have that kind visit from the boy. Life had provided those things to me; I had just followed the flow. I was beginning to see all these experiences as a gift from life.

7.

Disconnecting the
Panic Button

Mexico had been good for me, but it was now time to start my journey home. I headed back to the north and at day's end found a small lake off a dirt road where I could spend the night. It was so peaceful that I stayed there after my morning practices enjoying the water. Time came for my afternoon meditation session, so I hiked up a hill and found a secluded spot to start my yoga postures.

About halfway through my routine, I began to hear some voices in the distance. I started to get uncomfortable, but I was not about to give in to that scared person inside. I just relaxed more deeply into my yoga posture, and the anxiety subsided.

The next sound that startled me was that of a snorting horse a lot closer than the voices had been. I was convinced that these were the banditos. I soon heard both the voices and the horses a stone's throw from me. Relaxed was not exactly the word that came to mind. Scared, vulnerable, and terribly self-conscious was a much more accurate description of my state.

Everything in me wanted to end my yoga session immediately and open my eyes to see what danger I had gotten myself into. Well, everything except for the core of self-discipline I had developed for ridding myself of that scared person inside of me. The command of steel came from behind my fears: no way was I going to miss the opportunity to transcend all this inner commotion. I closed my eyes tighter as an act of defiance and took a deep breath. I demanded a state of relaxation in the midst of the drama.

When my usual set of yoga postures was complete, I normally sat for a half-hour meditation. I watched that voice pleading for permission to skip that step. After all, the horses had not gone anywhere. I could clearly hear their breathing right in front of me interspersed with the periodic whispering of their riders. There really was no decision to be made. I had clearly seen that it was this scared person inside of me who was holding me back from where I so desperately wanted to go. I needed to be free of him. So I took a deep breath and flowed into a full-lotus position. I began the *Mu* sound inside my belly in a vain attempt to drown out what the voice was trying to say. To me it was like an act of commitment: Which do you care about, outside or inside?

When I finally opened my eyes, I saw two horses right in front of me. They couldn't have been more than ten feet away. On top of the horses were two riders who looked more like ranch hands than banditos. They were smoking cigarettes, and one of them was sitting side-saddle facing the other rider. When they saw that I was back in their world, they began to talk to me in Spanish. I was somewhat surprised that I could understand most of what they were saying—and the very fact that they were talking to me was definitely a good thing. I began to feel relieved, and the series of events that transpired next left an indelible impression on my mind to stop letting that scared person run my life.

At some point in our interaction, the ranch hands asked if it was my van parked down by the lake. My mental voice immediately told me to be careful because they could rob me. I ignored that interlude and willingly reached my hand up when one of the riders offered to pull me onto his horse and ride me back to my van. I was a city boy; riding double on the back of a horse with a Mexican stranger while in my bathing suit was not an everyday occurrence for me. As I rode down the hill, a peace came over me from head to toe. This experience was so beautiful, and I would have missed it if I had listened to my scared self.

When we reached my van, the cowboy began telling me that he and others worked this land for a rich landowner. He said they were all very poor, and the landowner did not even allow them to fish in the lake. He pointed the way to where they lived and invited me to stop by before I left the next day. We said good-bye as though we had been friends for years, and they turned their horses and rode off.

I felt so open, so connected to the experience I was having. Though I was going through some very deep changes, I remember thanking life that night for such a special day. The pain and turmoil within me were beginning to subside, but the yearning for the absolute peace and silence continued to burn in my heart.

The next morning after my practices, I packed up to continue my journey northward. Before leaving, I decided to drive farther down the dirt road to see if I could find where the ranch hands lived. I came upon an area where there were fifteen to twenty adobe huts with thatched roofs. I had read about such things, but I had never actually seen a mud hut with a roof made of straw. Before I could decide if I wanted to go any farther, one of my new friends from the day before ran out to greet me.

I parked my van and followed the excited cowboy as he introduced his new American friend to the villagers. I was stunned by how primitive everything was. The huts were dirt floored and had nothing but square openings for windows. There were no doors in the door openings or windows in the window openings. Many of the people I met stared at me as though they had never seen an American before. I soon found out that many of them had not. I don't think the pestering voice in my head said one word for the hours I was there. It was all so new to me. It was so natural, so down to earth. I sat in a hut with women breast-feeding their babies. I had never seen that before. I noticed I actually felt ashamed that my culture had so distorted nature that natural things were no longer natural.

Once we were back outside, we continued our tour of the small village. When we approached my friend's hut, he asked me if I knew how to ride a horse. I told him it had been years, but that I had ridden before. What I didn't tell him was that the last time I rode I was twelve, and it was at summer camp with an English saddle. He then did the most unexpected thing. He handed me the reins to his horse and pointed to an open field. This was no time or place to be timid. I stuck my sandal into the stirrup and swung myself into the saddle, just as though I knew what I was doing. I had always thought it would be wild to gallop a horse across an open field. Somehow that dream was about to be realized in the middle of Mexico where I knew absolutely nobody. I got used to the horse while some of the villagers gathered to watch, and then I rode like the wind across an expansive field. I was really flying high, very exhilarated compared to the strict Zen discipline to which I had been holding myself.

I spent a few more hours discussing American life with some very inquisitive villagers and then began to bid them farewell. I was invited to stay for dinner, but it was time for my evening practices. I remembered that my friend had told me that they were not allowed to fish even though they were struggling for food. I went to my van and pulled out the large supply of brown rice and dried beans I had stored under the backseat. I handed them all over to the women preparing the food. The women were so appreciative that it almost made me cry. This stuff meant nothing to me and so much to them. This was another one of life's lessons I never forgot: the joy of helping people.

Before I drove off, they all surrounded my van to say good-bye. I had lived in silence and solitude with no human contact for almost a month—now I was a celebrity. How did this happen? To me there was no doubt about how it happened—I had let go of myself and something very special had followed. I was willing to face loneliness and fear and not grab for relief. Yet something happened on its own, without my doing it or even asking for it. The seeds of a great experiment were being planted. Was it possible that life had more to give us than we could ever take for ourselves?

8.

Unexpected Inspiration

I had grown a lot through my experiences in Mexico. Learning to embrace life as it unfolded around me was new to me, and the results had been very freeing. By the time I returned to Gainesville my heart and my mind were much more at peace. Problem was—I had no place to live. My last residence had been in the woods by the lime pit east of town, so I returned to that secluded setting and lived there in my van. All I needed in my life was solitude, the discipline of my ever-increasing practices, and a minimal amount of food.

I realized that the probability of finishing my doctoral degree was rapidly decreasing. I only had a few courses left, but then there were the qualifying exams as well as the dissertation. Nothing was left in me that wanted to be an economics professor. I wanted to explore inside, deep inside. The depths of my meditations were all I cared about.

The chairman of the Department of Economics, Dr. Goffman, was like a father to me. I loved and respected him a great deal, and he encouraged me to finish my degree. He thought I was just going through a phase in my youth, and I would come out of it soon. He kept me on my fellowship and pushed me to at least finish my coursework. Out of respect for him, I would drive into town periodically and go to class—but not very often.

I would eventually learn that everything in life has something to teach you and that it is all for your growth. But I was not ready to see that yet. To me, there was my meditation, and then there was everything else. Though I definitely wasn't seeing my schoolwork as relevant to my inner growth, I had a very illuminating experience associated with one of my courses.

The professor of the course was a respected economist and not at all the liberal type. I missed a lot of classes, and when I did show up, I was barefooted and in jeans. I doubt that I was his favorite student. One day he asked me if I actually expected to receive a good grade in the course. He explained that I had put out just enough effort to do well on the exams, but my absences and lack of participation in class did not provide the basis for a high grade. I knew we had a final paper left to write, so I told him I would put extra effort into that paper, and I'd appreciate it if he would base my grade solely on my exams and the quality of that paper. He said he would take it into consideration.

The time came to write the final paper for the course. I knew my mental state was not conducive to going to the library and trying to learn enough to write a great paper. I had been meditating a lot, and my mind was very still. No way was I going to spend days researching and thinking about the topic. I would have to find a different method if I was going to write this paper.

One evening, I gathered up a bunch of writing pads and a few pens. After meditation, I lit the kerosene lantern and sat at the fold-out table in my van. I began by telling myself that I really didn't care what grade I got in the class since I probably wouldn't finish my degree anyway. This removed any mental or emotional pressure. I then told myself to just start writing whatever I thought about the topic. I had no books to refer to, just the natural logic of a clear, unpressured mind. I began to write and thoughts began to flow. I did not worry about what I was writing or second-guess my thoughts. It was very much like meditation. I kept my personal self out of it completely and just let unbridled inspiration flow.

At some point in the process, a flash of inspiration welled up inside of me. I went from not knowing what I was going to do with the paper to knowing exactly what I was going to write. It was as though a cloud of knowing instantly formed back behind the quiet mind. It happened as fast and powerful as a flash of lightning. At first, no thoughts were involved. It was more of a feeling, just a definitive knowing that I now knew where the paper was going and how to get there. Then the thoughts began to form. They came slowly at first, then they poured into my mind. I still had to pull them together into a logical flow, but the seeds were all there. It was an amazing process to watch.

I wrote and I wrote. Notepad after notepad became filled with a totally logical presentation that began with a premise, laid out its argument, and ended with a conclusion. Along the way, there were graphs to present logical relationships, and there were references to facts I had previously read or heard in class. These facts would need to be polished and footnoted later, so I simply left space for them and kept on writing what was created in my mind. I stopped for nothing. There was no worrying or judgment of good or bad; I just allowed the process to unfold.

When artists create a work, they first get the inspiration, and then they bring it down to the physical plane. That process is exactly what happened to me that night alone in my van. The inspiration for the entire paper came all at once, and then my mind digested it and gave it form. Instead of a sculpture, a painting, or a symphony, my work of art was an economic treatise. It came from where art comes from, but the medium of expression was logical thinking instead of marble or paint. I had no idea where that spark of inspiration came from. I only knew that in the flash of a moment, I had all the material I needed to write a doctoral-level paper.

I took the next few days to clean up the rough draft, type it, and turn it in. The final typed paper was over thirty pages long. Not only did I receive an A for that course, but when my professor returned my paper, he asked me if I would consider doing my dissertation under him. I was humbled. As evidenced from this recounting forty years later, the experience that night had a profound effect on me. I had clearly seen the difference between creative inspiration and logical thought. I knew where thoughts came from, but where did inspiration come from? It came from a much deeper place than where I witnessed the thoughts. It came spontaneously, in total silence, with no effort or commotion. No matter how hard I might have tried, I could never have written that paper based solely on the efforts of my logical mind. I wondered if there was a way to tap into the brilliance of that inspiration on a regular basis. It would be years, but eventually I would learn that one can constantly live in that state of creative inspiration.

9

The Promised Land

It had been months since my deep meditation experience in the Ocala National Forest. The remnants of that experience were a constant flow of energy to the point between my eyebrows and a burning in my heart to go even deeper within. Neither of these forces subsided over time. In fact, the yearning to go deeper kept increasing on a daily basis. It was like having fallen madly in love and not being able to see your beloved. I began to contemplate completely dropping out and entering a life of solitude. My coursework was done, and nothing was forcing me to take my qualifying exams right away. Plus, by that time I was pretty certain that I would never take those exams.

I determined that I needed a place away from everything and everyone in order to become totally focused on my practices. I knew I couldn't just keep camping by the lime pit forever, but I wasn't ready to start looking for a secluded place of my own. I decided to just keep my eyes open to see if something would show up by itself.

Something did.

I was filling up my van one day, when out of the blue the gas station attendant asked me where I lived. I told him that I had been living in my van for a while but was hoping to find a piece of land in the country. He said he had come across a beautiful place northwest of Gainesville that had five-acre lots for sale. I got directions and went on my way.

A few days later, I drove out to the place and found April Gift

Estates. It was in a heavily wooded area about ten miles north of town, and it consisted of twenty-one five-acre lots and a couple of dirt roads. Very few lots had been sold, and I didn't see a single person the entire time I toured. The place was so peaceful and natural that I drove around almost in a trance. It was just perfect.

I soon came upon a couple of adjoining lots that were part woods and part field. This was exactly what I had wanted. I parked my car and walked through the woods onto the interior field. The feeling of going from the woods to sudden openness was unbelievable. There was a rush of light and a feeling of expansiveness.

I walked up a rolling hill to the fence on the north side of the property. The property bordered a beautiful pasture that sloped down to a woods-lined stream. The entire north side of the lot overlooked that breathtaking view. It reminded me of how Homer described the Elysian Fields. I meandered back into the woods and found a spot under a tree where I could see the interior field open in front of me and the beautiful pastureland to my right. The woods were quiet and felt protecting. It was like being in a womb. The moment I sat down, I was drawn into deep meditation. The moment I came back, I knew I was home.

I had never bought a piece of land before, but I did have some funds. When I graduated from college, my father had given me what remained in my college account. He wanted me to take full responsibility for my postgraduate education. Since I did both my master's degree and my doctorate work under full fellowship, I had been able to save almost all of the $15,000 he had given me. It was now time to spend it.

I decided to try to buy both of the lots that included the interior field. That would give me plenty of seclusion. Before contacting the owner, I picked a maximum number that I was willing to pay for the ten acres. The number was significantly less than the asking price, but I told myself that if the seller wouldn't come down to my price, it wasn't meant to be. I was completely at peace with either outcome. As it turned out, that sense of detachment gave me the edge I needed to successfully negotiate for the lots. I succeeded in the purchase, but I didn't feel a sense of joy. What I felt was a sense of resolute determination. What lay ahead of me was not going to be easy. I had already committed so much of myself to exploring what was beyond me—now I was going to commit everything.

10.

Building a Sacred Hut

Bob Gould and I had been friends since my first days of high school. We had both moved to Florida from up north and were the new kids entering tenth grade. We bonded immediately and remained good friends all the way through college. Bob was the handy type, the kind of kid who always excelled in shop class. When it came time to build a meditation hut on my land, he jumped at the opportunity.

Neither Bob nor I had ever built anything like a hut to actually live in. I was good with my hands and had been a sports car mechanic while in high school. But to build a small house, Bob and I were way out of our league. We reached out to a college friend, Bobby Altman. Bobby's credentials were not that he had actually built a house before, but that he had just finished his master's degree in architecture. At least he had the theory of how to design and build something. How hard could it be to build a small hut where I could go into solitude for a while?

Apparently, Bobby Altman didn't think it would be hard at all. He quickly designed plans for the hut, which included a balsa wood model. I remember the first time I saw his design. I literally thought he was crazy. This was not just a small, simple, one-person hut for meditation. It was a wedged-shaped house with a stunning front of glass that spanned sixteen feet wide and rose twenty feet high. To be perfectly honest, I had been envisioning more of a box with a door and a few windows. How were three college grads, who had never built anything before, going to build this?

Bobby Altman insisted the house was going to be easy to build. I wasn't so sure, but Bob Gould was all for it. He thought it would be a fun challenge for the three of us to live on the land in tents and build it. I remember that I didn't see it that way. I already had a full-time challenge—getting back to my beloved place of absolute stillness and peace. But if I had to build this architecturally designed masterpiece of a meditation hut to get there—so be it.

We jumped right in with the abandonment of reason that belongs only to young hippies and crazy people. It was an amazing experience. I had very little money left to build Bobby Altman's chalet. To keep costs to a minimum, both Bobs agreed that we could use rough-sawn lumber instead of the finished lumber you buy at a lumberyard. As fate would have it, there was a sawmill just a few miles down the highway from my land: Griffis Lumber & Sawmill. James Griffis and his wife were real southern country folk, not longhairs like the three of us. We got sideways looks from pretty much everyone whenever we went to pick up lumber. Aside from our hair, we stood out because of what we were ordering. We started with the eleven cypress columns that would form the support structure of the house—at twenty-nine feet, you might as well call them trees. James Griffis allowed us to hand select the straightest trees right off the logging truck when it arrived. We got to watch workers strap each of the trees to the giant mill and cut them down to six inches per side, give or take half an inch. It was a real back-to-the-earth feeling watching the actual trees being turned into the backbone of your house.

In time, Mr. Griffis began to open up to us. One day he invited the three of us to dinner at his house, which was adjacent to the mill. This was a big deal since we had been living in tents and cooking what we could over an open fire. It was particularly special for me because I had been living out of my van or in a tent for almost half a year. It wasn't just a matter of a home-cooked meal; just going into a real house was going to be a novelty for me.

The Griffises' house was a warm country home. The walls were pecky cypress, milled long ago on-site. Mrs. Griffis had cooked up a southern meal with plenty of vegetables, since she had heard that I was a vegetarian. The conversations were warm and friendly, and it really felt as though we were all family. At one point, Mr. Griffis said something I will never forget. He said, "Before we met you three, we used to think that hippies were the dirtiest, filthiest things on Earth. You know, we've really come to love you boys." It was another one of those beautiful moments that started me thinking—where were all these unbelievable experiences coming from? Somehow, deeply touching experiences kept coming from the most unexpected places. It was really starting to blow me away.

As days turned into weeks, the house began to take shape. Once the outside siding was up, you could really begin to feel the inside space. Bobby Altman then posed a question I had never thought of—which of us was going to do the electrical wiring? Though I had never done such a thing, I volunteered. Bobby handed me a small book on electrical wiring from one of his courses and left me on my own. His confidence in my ability to do the entire electrical system for the house rather astounded me. But if he thought I could do it, then I could—and I did. A great spiritual teacher once said, "Every day bite off more than you can chew, and chew it." Life was teaching me some very important lessons.

We laid pinewood floors throughout the house, put cedar decks in both the front and back, and hired a plumber to install exposed, cast-iron plumbing pipes for the bathroom area. By then, the house had taken on a life of its own. We had put our hearts and souls into building that house, and we were very proud of what we had accomplished. To me, it had started out as a project to build a quick, simple meditation hut, and it turned into a one-of-a-kind life experience. But it wasn't the one I longed for. All I really wanted was to go into solitude and work on my heart's only desire—absolute peace, stillness, and freedom. With the house finished, the time for that work had finally arrived.

November 1971: All I wanted was a tiny meditation hut—just look at what life gave us to build!

House finished—time for solitude.

11

Get Thee to a Monastery

I moved into my new house in November 1971. I remember it was November because just before I moved in, my sister, Kerry, and her husband came up from Miami to visit me for Thanksgiving. This was very brave of them, considering they were regular folk. Harvey was a successful accountant, and he and Kerry were used to a nice house and comfortable living conditions. When they showed up, I was busy finishing the final checklist before moving out of my van and into the house. Harvey helped me install the last two windows and then insisted on having Thanksgiving dinner with me. That meant they joined me sitting outside on rocks and cooking what we could on an open fire. Personally, I think they had come up to check on me to see if I was still halfway sane. I had been without a phone number for a long time, and I'm sure my family must have been concerned about me.

Once Kerry and Harvey left, I was glad to be alone again with my beautiful new house. All I had wanted was a simple place to fully focus on my meditations. What I got was a gift from the invisible hand that had taken over my life. That's what I called it back then—the invisible hand. From the beginning of my awakening, I had inwardly begged for help in knowing who I was, the one who was watching the voice of the mind. From that point forward, it was as though something had reached down and grabbed me by the ponytail and begun to pull me up. My whole outer life had been ripped away from me in the blink of an eye. In its place I had been shown the beauty and peace of an inner state that was beyond anything I had ever imagined. That touch of the beyond had lit my heart aflame. I had a fire burning in the pit of my being that never left me alone—even for a moment. It was like a beckoning, a calling to come home. At that stage of my awakening, the only way I knew how to get back was to willfully push my way through myself with the intense discipline of Zen meditation. As I sat at the threshold of the door that opened into the beautiful place that life had given me to do this work, I reverently bowed my head. This was my temple, my monastery, and I vowed to use it well.

I was very surprised to find that the monastic lifestyle came quite naturally to me. I awoke every morning at 3:00 a.m. and sat for a few hours of meditation. I would then do contemplative walking out on the fields. In those early days, I was still holding on to the concept that it was all about concentration and focus. When I walked, I would become acutely aware of every step I took and every movement of my body. This helped to prolong the peace I felt from my morning meditations. I would then do yoga postures outside until it was time for my noon meditation. I held the rope of self-discipline very tightly, every day. It was an extremely strict lifestyle, very different from anything I had ever experienced. But just as an athlete is willing to give everything, every day and night, to train for the Olympics, so I was willing to give everything, every moment, to drop the part of me that was holding me back from where I so desperately wanted to go.

It didn't take long before I noticed that food had a major effect on my practices. The less I ate, the easier it was to fall into a meditative state. So I tested the limits of how far I could go without eating. The balance I reached was to eat a small dinner salad every other day and fast in between. My intention was to give up everything possible that pulled my attention outward. This would allow me to more fully focus on the deeper inner states.

My nighttime routine began at sunset. Somehow the setting sun strongly affected the force that pulled me into meditation. I was always on my meditation pillow before the sun started setting. After a few hours of meditation, I would make my way upstairs to go to sleep. I had no alarm clock; I awoke naturally at 3:00 a.m. every morning to start the regimen again.

I don't know where I got the idea that if I held the rope tight enough, my lower self would go away and leave me alone. But that is how I lived for about a year and a half. The part of me that had dominated my entire previous way of life had no place in my new life. There were no perks for him, and every day he fought back less and less. The noisy, demanding personal part of me didn't go away—he just began to resign himself to the intense discipline. I thought it was working, but I would soon come to see that I was very wrong.

12

When the Disciple Is Ready, the Master Appears

Other than for schoolwork, reading books had never played a major role in my life. But just as *Three Pillars of Zen* had shown up exactly when I was ready for it, so another book had found its way to me just before I moved into my house. It was given to me by Bob Merrill, a friend of mine who, like me, was very much into yoga and meditation.

One day while I was still living in my van, Bob gave me the book called *Autobiography of a Yogi* by Paramahansa Yogananda, a holy man from India. I remember trying to start this book the evening Bob had given it to me, but after a few pages I had to put it down. Not because I didn't like it, but because each word I read kept drawing me into such a deep meditative state that I couldn't continue reading. I tried again the next night. The same thing happened. I didn't understand what was going on, but I was certainly intrigued by the experience. I decided to pack the book away until I moved into my new house. Now that I had moved into the house and started my intense meditative lifestyle, it was time to read this mysterious book.

Chapter after chapter transported me into a world that should have been very foreign to me. But because of the transformative events that had been happening to me, I could at least relate to the Indian saint's life story. It became very clear to me—I had merely stuck my toe into the ocean Yogananda was swimming in. He was a master of the entire field of knowledge and experience I was seeking. I could feel it to the core of my being. Yogananda had gone far beyond my beyond and had never fully come back. He had learned to exist in that state, yet still be present interacting with the world. I had found my teacher.

Even though I felt an immediate sense of relief that I was no longer alone on my inner journey, some areas of tension had to be worked out. To begin with, the word *God* was not part of my everyday vocabulary. Yogananda not only used the word as freely as his breath flowed, but he used it with a sense of intense devotion that took your breath away. Yogananda's passion showed most in the songs that he wrote:

My heart's aflame and my soul's afire—Just for You, You, You, Just You.

Interestingly, I could relate to that. Since I had touched that beauteous place deep inside of me, my heart was aflame too. In fact, I had lost interest in everything else. I only wanted to meditate my way back beyond myself. I could relate to God as associated with that place hidden deep inside of me. My study of Zen taught me that Buddha passed through absolute stillness and peace on his way into *nirvana*. I had heard that Christ said that the *Kingdom is within you,* and I was aware that the Bible talked about *a peace beyond all understanding.* I knew about such a place inside of me where the peace was so deep that it had completely transformed my entire life.

Another word that I couldn't relate to at first was *Spirit.* I thought this was a Christian word, yet Yogananda used it all the time. He spoke of invoking the Spirit and feeling it pulsate through him. He related times when he held up his hands and felt the Spirit move into and out of them. Could he be referring to that powerful flow of energy I had been experiencing since my very deep meditation? I often felt that field of energy flow from the point between my eyebrows, down my arms, and out the center of my palms. Could Spirit be another word for this inner energy flow, and could that focal point between my eyebrows be the location of what Yogananda kept calling the *Third Eye* or *Spiritual Eye*? More and more I began to realize that I could personally relate to Yogananda's teachings.

Autobiography of a Yogi changed my view about everything that had been happening to me. Once I finished reading that book, God was no longer just a word to me. It represented where I wanted to go. I had begun this journey by wanting to know who I was who was watching the mental voice. I now realized that the great saints and masters of all the religious traditions had gone beyond their personal self to find their spiritual self. Yogananda called it *self-realization*. What a perfect term for all I was about at that point of my life. I wanted to realize the nature of the one who watches—my true, innermost self.

Bob Merrill had told me that he received lessons from *Self-Realization Fellowship,* the organization Yogananda had founded in America. Yogananda had left the body in 1952, but he had been kind enough to leave his teachings behind in the form of weekly lessons. I had heard of a mail-order bride but never a mail-order guru. I signed up for the lessons immediately and integrated them into my regular practices. I remember that around that time I decided to read the Bible. I had never read the New Testament before. I found it very inspiring, and so much of the teachings were completely aligned with what I had been experiencing in meditation. For example, there was the notion that you have to die to be reborn. That is exactly what I had been trying to do, die of the personal to be reborn in the spiritual. I put pictures of Christ and Yogananda on the altar where I meditated. Some very great beings had walked this path before me. I wanted to learn from them. I was just starting to realize that I couldn't walk the path alone—I needed some help.

Section II

. . . .

The Great

Experiment Begins

13.

The Experiment
of a Lifetime

Thus far my entire path to inner freedom was focused around my meditations. That was where I went to become filled with a deep sense of peace and serenity. And it was working, to a degree. I could sit for hours with a beautiful flow of energy lifting me upward, but I couldn't break through to where I longed to go. Furthermore, the personal mind always returned once I got up and became active. I needed help, and it came one day in a flash of realization. It dawned on me that perhaps I'd been going about this in the wrong way. Instead of trying to free myself by constantly quieting the mind, perhaps I should be asking why the mind is so active. What is the motivation behind all the mental chatter? If that motivation were to be removed, the struggle would be over.

This realization opened the door for an entirely new and exciting dimension to my practices. As I explored it inwardly, the first thing I noticed was that most of the mental activity revolved around my likes and dislikes. If my mind had a preference toward or against something, it actively talked about it. I could see that it was these mental preferences that were creating much of the ongoing dialogue about how to control everything in my life. In a bold attempt to free myself from all that, I decided to just stop listening to all the chatter about my personal preferences, and instead, start the willful practice of accepting what the flow of life was presenting me. Perhaps this change in focus would quiet things down inside.

I started this new practice with something very simple, the weather. Could it really be so hard to just let it rain when it rains and be sunny when it's sunny without complaining about it? Apparently the mind can't do it:

Why did it have to rain today? It always rains when I don't want it to. It had all week to rain; it's just not fair.

I simply replaced all that meaningless noise with:

Look how beautiful; it's raining.

I found these practices of acceptance very powerful, and they definitely served to quiet the mind. So I decided to push the envelope and broaden the range of events I would learn to accept. I clearly remember deciding that from now on if life was unfolding in a certain way, and the only reason I was resisting it was because of a personal preference, I would let go of my preference and let life be in charge.

Clearly, these were uncharted waters for me. Where would I end up? If my preferences were not leading me, what would happen to me? These questions did not scare me; they fascinated me. I didn't want to be in charge of my life; I wanted to be free to soar far beyond myself. I began to see this as a great experiment. What would happen to me if I just inwardly surrendered my resistance and let the flow of life be in charge? The rules of the experiment were very simple: If life brought events in front of me, I would treat them as if they came to take me beyond myself. If my personal self complained, I would use each opportunity to simply let him go and surrender to what life was presenting me. This was the birth of what I came to call "the surrender experiment," and I was totally prepared to see where it would take me.

You may think that only a madman would make such a decision. But, in truth, I had already experienced some amazing things that the flow of life had done. I had witnessed firsthand what happened when I let go and followed the subtle events that led me to the hills of Mexico and then to those wonderful experiences with the Mexican villagers. When I got back to the States, I had been led to my beautiful new property, and look what happened with the house. I just wanted to build a simple hut, and that turned into an unexpectedly rich experience. It was clear to me that I had not done these things—*they had happened to me*. In fact, if I had not let go of my initial mental resistance, none of them could have happened. I had gone through most of my life thinking I knew what was good for me, but life itself seemed to know better. I was now going to test that presumption of nonrandomness to the max. I was willing to roll the dice and let the flow of life be in charge.

14.

Life Takes Charge

Surrendering to the flow of life may have seemed like a bold move, but the truth is, I wasn't all that exposed to life's challenges. After all, I was spending most of my days alone on my land in quietude. There was one exception, however. I was officially still in graduate school until I completed my qualifying exams and dissertation. That meant I remained on a fellowship at the university and was responsible for teaching one course a semester in either micro- or macroeconomics. My classes generally met three days a week for an hour. I would do my morning and noon yoga practices, run into town to teach, and then run right back out to the land. I doubt I was a real joy to be around in those days—I was completely unsociable. Unless a student had a question after class, I would do my best not to get into conversations. I always wore the same clothes: jeans and a long-sleeved denim shirt. My hair was pulled back in a ponytail, and I was either in sandals or barefoot. This might not seem extreme for the philosophy department, but these were junior-level courses in a southern business school. The department tolerated me only because I was a very popular teacher, and my students did really well on the departmental exams.

I will recount one specific class session that was over the top. My challenge to myself was to see whether I could drive into town, teach the class, and return home while keeping my mind reasonably still. To do that I had to practice maintaining a meditative state at many points throughout the day. I would do yoga on the field before I left and do some controlled breathing exercises in my van before going to class. I would even pause to quiet my mind while standing in front of the class before I started and completed a lecture. On this particular day, I drove in, did some breathing, and walked into a large lecture hall full of students. For some reason they started whistling catcalls when I walked in. It took me a moment to come down to earth enough to realize that when I had gotten off the yoga mat out at my place, I had slipped into my jeans but had forgotten to put on a shirt. I was standing there barefooted and half naked. It didn't disturb me—I just asked the class whether they wanted to cancel today's session or have me go ahead and teach it. The response was unanimous, so I gave the lecture on macroeconomics without regard to my attire, or lack thereof.

Month after month went by while I was adhering to my strict meditation lifestyle. I was supposed to be using my time to prepare for my doctoral qualifying exams. Needless to say, I had not opened a single book, and I had no intention of doing so. I was done with that part of my life. Or so I thought.

One day, after I finished teaching my economics class, Dr. Goffman met me in the hallway and said he wanted to talk to me. The voice in my head immediately told me that now I was in trouble. He was still chairman of the department, and for sure he had heard about the no-shirt incident. As usual, that voice was wrong.

Dr. Goffman proceeded to tell me that he had received a call from the governor's office in Tallahassee. Apparently, the powers that be had decided to build one of Florida's leading community colleges in Gainesville. To do so they would need a powerful leader who could not only handle the educational responsibilities, but also be in charge of fund-raising and financial management. With that in mind, the committee had selected one of the state's leading bankers to be the president of the newly expanded Santa Fe Community College. During the entire time Dr. Goffman was talking, my mind kept saying, *Why is he telling me this? What has it got to do with me? I should be getting back out to my land.*

I soon got my answers. It seemed that Florida law required the president of a community college to have a doctoral degree. The banker the committee had chosen, Alan Robertson, did not have his

Ph.D. So what did they decide to do? Help him earn his doctorate by partnering him with a top doctoral student who had a similar academic background. As amazing as it seems, the doctoral student they chose was me.

The voice in my head went nuclear. I watched it screaming inside, *No! I can't do that. I've dropped out of all this. I need to devote my time to my practices. There is no way I'm going to start pulling down all my old economics textbooks—I'm done with that.* In the midst of all that protest, I remembered my recent commitment to surrender to what life brought before me. That voice I was watching was not my spiritual adviser; it was my spiritual burden. This was the perfect opportunity to get it out of the driver's seat.

Meanwhile, Dr. Goffman was waiting for a response. But the words of acceptance I was trying to utter refused to leave my lips. Finally, I heard myself say out loud, "Yes, I would be glad to help out. I will tutor him."

In that one moment, the die had been cast. This great experiment in surrender had truly begun.

I was no longer in charge of my life.

15.

The Prince and the Pauper

Tutoring Alan Robertson really didn't change my lifestyle all that much. We arranged our schedules such that whenever I went into town to teach, I would spend a few hours with Alan after class. We met in the president's office at the old Santa Fe campus downtown near the university. We were quite the pair. Alan was a very successful, three-piece-suit banker, and I was a ponytailed yogi in denim jeans and sandals. I had no idea what to expect, but Alan turned out to be an exceptionally warm and open-minded person. He was also very grateful for my help.

This is not to say that there weren't some awkward moments. The first culture clash was regarding payment for my services. I told him that I didn't want to be paid for tutoring him. He insisted, but I refused. He went on to reason with me that he was a successful banker who was now president of a college, and I was a student living off a $250-a-month fellowship. That was true enough, and it was also true that I had spent everything I had buying the land and building my house. Nonetheless, I was tutoring him as an act of surrender to the flow of life, and I didn't want to be paid.

In time, Alan accepted our relationship on nonbusiness terms, and we became good friends. Sometimes he would come out to my land to study, and we would take long walks together. He enjoyed learning about my unique way of life, and I enjoyed meeting the very special man behind the banker's suit. A few times I even accepted his wife's invitation to have dinner at their home. I began to see my entire relationship with Alan as another one of life's magical gifts, despite my initial resistance.

Alan had progressed enough toward his doctorate to sit for his qualifying exams. He surprised me when he proposed that I go ahead and take mine also. I had no interest in doing so, especially since we had only prepared for two of my three major areas of study. But I surrendered to his wishes. I signed up to take the two exams we had studied for and planned to put the third off to another time—if at all. When I received notice back from the university, the administration had mistakenly signed me up for all three exams. Now what was I supposed to do, surrender to that?

I started observing myself to see why taking the third exam threatened me so much. I had no intention of actually finishing my degree, so why did it matter? What I discovered was that it was simply the fear of failing in the eyes of others. I knew that if I sat for my written exam in public finance, a field I was completely unprepared for, I would fail miserably. That prospect of failure disturbed me and set the inner voice on a nonstop dialogue about how to avoid the exam. What an opportunity to get rid of that part of me. I no longer saw the administration's mistake as a problem. I saw it as a challenge to further let go of myself. So I decided to take all three exams and willingly accept the experience of failing the third one.

The first two exams went very smoothly. I had done a lot of work with Alan in these areas, so I knew the material reasonably well. As the day for the third exam approached, I strengthened my heart for the inevitable. I would march into that exam and willingly let a part of my ego die a painful death.

What ended up happening changed me for the rest of my life. The day before the exam, I allowed myself to pull down the public finance textbook for the first time. I took the large book outside and sat it beside me as I did my yoga. When I finished my postures, I felt quiet, peaceful, and totally prepared to face the next day's ordeal. As if to examine the sword I was about to fall upon, I opened the book to an arbitrary place. I read both pages that appeared before me. I performed this ritual three times before holding the book up to the heavens as a sign of my willingness to surrender.

The next day, I watched closely to see what that voice would have to say. I was surprised to be feeling very peaceful about the upcoming event. After my morning meditation, I pulled down the book one more time and opened to an arbitrary page. It turned out to be one of the three places I had opened to the day before. I reviewed the complex chart on that page and put the book back on the shelf for the last time.

Later that morning, I parked outside the business school and meditated for a while before going in. I still felt very quiet inside. There was just a sense of peaceful resignation. I remember feeling I had passed the real test—I had proven that I was capable of deeply surrendering if life presented me with something I really did not want to do.

I went upstairs to the economics department, and the administrative assistant handed me the exam. As I took it from her hands, I glanced over the six essay questions of which I had to answer three. I immediately froze, and tears began to well up in my eyes. Three of the questions were exactly about the three places where I had arbitrarily opened the book the day before. I was stunned. I stood there for a long time unable to even take a breath.

How could this be? It had happened again. In the name of transcending myself, I had surrendered and willingly faced my personal fears. Then at the last moment, instead of certain hell, I was lifted up to heaven.

I went into the designated room and wrote and wrote. The seeds of inspiration were very fresh in my mind. I was even able to reproduce and embellish upon the chart I had opened to twice. I turned in the notebooks and headed home in a very different state of mind than I had expected. Driving to the exam, I had felt as though life was asking me to willingly let a part of me die that day. But now I realized that life was asking me to get out of the way and let her do her thing. I was so glad I had been willing to take that risk.

Days later I was called in by Dr. Goffman and complimented on the excellence of my public finance exam. This recognition from the chairman of the department should have pleased me, but instead it actually made me feel guilty. I recounted the whole story and asked if I had somehow done something wrong. Dr. Goffman got up, placed his hand on my shoulder, and told me to stop trying to be so humble. He then directed me out of his office.

16.

Following the Invisible
into the Unknown

By the spring of 1972, through no intention of my own, I had completed both the course work and the qualifying exams for my doctorate. All that was left was writing a dissertation. I knew that would never happen, so I didn't give it a second thought. My meditations and yoga were my entire life.

Though I had advanced considerably in my practices, I still felt something was holding me back. I began to believe that the answer was the practice of Kriya yoga, a special meditation technique taught by Yogananda. The problem was that you had to receive the lessons for a year before becoming eligible. I decided to ask Self-Realization Fellowship for early initiation into the practice of Kriya yoga.

In those days, I hardly ever got mail. So I was surprised some weeks later when I received two letters on the same day: one from Self-Realization Fellowship, and the other from some organization I'd never heard of. I was very excited to learn the fellowship's response, so I opened that letter first. My heart dropped to my feet. I'd have to wait another six months to receive the Kriya technique. There was not much I could do about it but let go of my reaction. I took a deep breath and opened the other letter. With one glance, all my disappointment faded into emptiness. Inside was a flyer that said in big, bold letters:

**Receive Kriya This Summer from a
Direct Disciple of Paramahansa Yogananda**

I was stunned once again. I had never heard of these people. They appeared to be an established yoga community in California, but there was no way that they could know me or have gotten my address. I was a hermit living in the woods of Florida. How could these two perfectly intertwined letters end up in my mailbox at the same time?

Regardless of the answer to that intriguing question, I knew where I was supposed to go that summer—to a spiritual community in Northern California. It's not hard to follow the guidance when it's that obvious. But my commitment to letting life be in charge from now on would face a few more challenges before I left for my adventure out west.

A short time after the incident with the letters, Dr. Goffman contacted me to let me know that Alan Robertson was trying to reach me. I hadn't talked to Alan since we had both passed our exams. I got in touch with him and learned that they had completed construction of the new Santa Fe Community College campus. Alan was staffing up for the opening classes and wanted me to teach there, even if only on a part-time basis. I became very quiet. I had absolutely no interest in teaching at Santa Fe Community College or any other institution. My only intention was to just keep increasing my spiritual practices until I could remain merged in the beautiful places I had discovered within. I tried to tell Alan this, but he didn't want to listen. Finally, he said, "I am not asking you, I'm telling you." My mouth became dry as I uttered the words my heart did not want to say: "Yes, sir. I will teach there on a part-time basis. What do I need to do?"

Surrender—what an amazingly powerful word. It often engenders the thought of weakness and cowardice. In my case, it required all the strength I had to be brave enough to follow the invisible into the unknown. And that is exactly what I was doing. It's not that surrender gave me clarity about where I was going—I had no idea where it would lead me. But surrender did give me clarity in one essential area: my personal preferences of like and dislike were not going to guide my life. By surrendering the hold those powerful forces had on me, I was allowing my life to be guided by a much more powerful force, life itself.

By that stage of my growth, I could see that the practice of sur-render was actually done in two, very distinct steps: first, you let go of the personal reactions of like and dislike that form inside your mind and heart; and second, with the resultant sense of clarity, you simply look to see what is being asked of you by the situation unfolding in front of you. What would you be doing if you weren't being influenced by the reactions of like or dislike? Following that deeper guidance will take your life in a very different direction from where your preferences would have led you. That is the clearest I can explain my surrender experiment, and it became the foundation of both my spiritual and worldly life.

17

My First Job Interview

I had been in school most of my life, and except for my stint as a sports car mechanic after classes in high school, I had only worked summer jobs. I had never been on a real job interview before. Alan arranged for me to meet with a program director to discuss my position at the college.

On the day of the interview, I arrived in my normal attire: jeans, a denim shirt, and sandals. The downtown campus of Santa Fe had been pretty liberal, but I had no idea how things were at the new campus with Alan as president. The program director began by asking me what I would like to teach. I figured I was supposed to give an honest answer. I told her I would like to teach what I had been learning about that voice inside your head. I wanted students to understand that they don't have to listen to that incessant chatter; they have the freedom to come from a much deeper place inside themselves. I also told her that I would like to teach students that they are sitting on a tiny planet spinning through space, and they should be enjoying the journey. To my amazement, her response was to say that the only course available that could allow such a curriculum was an entry-level social science class. The course was required for all freshmen, and a teacher was still needed for one-third of the classes. She explained that teaching those classes would amount to a half-time position at the college. I accepted the position, and she scheduled me to teach my first class in September when the new campus officially opened.

What a flow of events! First life tells me to go to California for the summer; now she's telling me what to do when I come back. It

was all unfolding by itself. I was just along for the ride. I really had
no idea what I was going to teach in that class come September. I had
never taught what I'd been learning to anyone, let alone a whole class.
My personal self began feeling insecure about the whole thing. To
straighten him out, I laid down the ground rules: there would not be a
single thought about the classes or what would be taught in them until
it was time to enter the classroom. I intended to walk into the first
class with a completely empty mind. I wanted it to be like the time I
wrote that paper completely by inspiration. We'll just go into the class
and see what comes out.

With these intrusions from the outside world starting to steal small
chunks of my time, I all the more cherished being alone on my land.
Nevertheless, people had a way of finding me, despite my best efforts
to protect my solitude. So it was with Sandy Boone, a woman who was
into Buddhist meditation and spending time outdoors. I don't recall
where she came from, but one day she showed up and started taking walks on my property. She was careful to respect my privacy; she
just wanted to be in nature and meditate outdoors. That was okay
until she asked if she could pitch her tent at the far end of the property
to do some meditation. I didn't want to allow that, but who was I to
stop someone from meditating? Eventually she got bold enough to ask
if she could join me for meditation on Sunday mornings, just for an
hour. I clearly remember granting her request solely because the voice
in my head was so resistant to it.

In time, Sandy began to bring a few friends with her for the Sunday morning meditations. At first it was three, then six, then ten. I
didn't like that at all, but I had no right to stop it. I often just stayed in
meditation upstairs while my guests met downstairs. Thus the notion
of Sunday morning services at Mickey's started in the spring of 1972—
a tradition that has continued every Sunday for over forty years.

Meanwhile, summer was approaching, and it was time to begin
preparing for my trip to California. I figured I would camp in my van
at the spiritual community for three or four weeks and then come back
home in time for classes. The drive out there took me about ten days

because I continued all my meditation sessions along the way. When I arrived at the community, I found a very rural setting with a large expanse of land and many small, rustic cabins. The people seemed like back-to-the-earth-type folks, and I fit right in. During registration, I noticed special name tags for guests who wanted to practice silence. I had no interest in meeting people or making new friends—that would just be a distraction to my inner work. So I decided to use the trip to step up my practices to an even stricter level: I would remain in total silence during my visit.

There were no available campgrounds near their temple area, so I simply parked my van in the nearest dirt parking lot. That is where I would live for a few weeks. After getting situated, I began doing my afternoon yoga and meditation session in their temple. Though I was accustomed to being alone, I immediately realized that I would be fine here for a while. These people understood what I was into and would leave me to my practices. I continued fasting three times a week, and when I ate my salad, I always sat alone. I was not exactly the social type, but I did attend evening meditation and chanting programs in the temple. In fact, that was where I was first exposed to Eastern chanting. Because I was in silence I didn't chant, but I could feel the upliftment of the energy in the room.

I would have gone on like that during my entire stay—if it were not for a dream I had. I hardly ever dreamed, and when I did, the dreams didn't seem to have any deep significance. One night I had a phenomenal, lucid dream that had a profound effect on me. I dreamed that I was doing intensely focused Zen walking. I was very consciously placing one foot in front of the other as I slowly headed toward the mouth of a cave. I entered the cave without incident and proceeded into the darkness that stretched before me. When it became very dark, I picked up a wooden torch mounted on the side of the cave. I lit it and continued as before. I noticed that the air was getting thinner and thinner the deeper I went into the cave. There was an almost frighteningly strong sense of purpose: I was going to explore deep into this unknown cave until I found what I was looking for. Nothing was going to stop me.

I began to see a faint light far off in the distance. Not a single thought passed through my mind, yet I intuitively knew that was where I was going. As I approached, I could see that the light was coming from above and shining down into the cave. The closer I got to the source of the light, the thinner the air became. I could hardly breathe. But I kept on going. The experience was similar to what had been happening in my practices. In my meditations, the deeper I went, the more my breath would slow down—until, eventually, it would naturally stop flowing. I don't know how long I would stay in that breathless state, but I would come back and gasp for air. At some point, my walk through this cave felt just like that stage of my meditations.

I was almost there. I could see the streaming rays of light pouring onto the cave floor just in front of me. I felt as though I would collapse from the lack of oxygen, but I found the will to take that final step into the light. In an instant, I was completely bathed in a flood of blinding light. I turned upward to climb into the light, but my hands hit a metal grate on the roof of the cave. There was no way out from here.

Not a thought entered my mind. Not a sigh left my lips. With the same steely sense of purpose that had led me into this cave, I turned and began to walk back out. There was simply the knowing—I would have to find another way.

18

Letting Go of the Rope

I awoke from that dream a changed person. My way of thinking had been transformed at a very profound level. For the first time, I questioned whether more and more discipline was going to take me where I so desperately wanted to go. Sitting alone in my van that morning, I knew the answer was no. My path to true freedom was subtler than simply requiring a tighter grip.

Something much wiser than me had reached into my psyche that night and rearranged my entire relationship with myself. I no longer saw the lower aspect of myself, with all his personal issues and melodramas, as the enemy that had to be destroyed. I looked at him now with a new understanding. I needed to use all these disturbed personal energies for my ascent. It was perfectly clear to me that since he was the problem, he was also the solution. I actually felt a tinge of compassion toward that struggling person within me. I would later come to learn that the *Bhagavad Gita* says that one should raise the self with Self, not trample down the self. I had been trampling down my personal self in the name of getting free from his humanness. I now needed to learn how to raise those energies up to assist me on the journey.

I left my van and walked in the direction of the temple building. I was feeling much lighter and more open. I felt like I wanted to unbind myself and spread my wings. But there was something that I needed to do first. Since the beginning of my mental disciplines, I had imagined a room inside my mind where I would take my personal self to meditate. It was a room with giant wooden doors for entry and solid glass for walls. What made this room so special was that the glass walls looked out upon the entire universe. Sitting in the lone meditation seat, one could see Earth suspended in the darkness of space. In the distance were stars and galaxies floating in the infinite. Whenever Mickey had a problem, I took him there to chill out. I even used to play with leaving him there. I wanted him always to be quiet, and I wanted him always to remember that all his experiences were happening on a tiny speck of dirt floating through infinite space.

That morning when I stopped on my way to the temple, I closed my eyes and opened the giant wooden doors to that very special room. The person I had left sitting on the meditation seat immediately straightened himself up. As I approached him, he became more disciplined and focused. In drastic contrast to how strict I had been in the past, I reached my hand out to him in a kind and caring manner and said, "You can come out now." What followed that utterance makes me ashamed to this day for thinking this practice was some sort of an innocent mind game. The moment I said those words, I experienced an emotional release the intensity of which I had never imagined possible. Tears poured from my eyes, and my legs completely buckled beneath me. My heart broke open as though some major event had taken place that allowed for a lifetime's worth of relief.

Once this cathartic release had run its course, I realized something I will never forget: that scared, troubled person in there whom I had been watching and judging was indeed a person. The psyche is a person with feelings and thoughts, hopes, fears, and dreams. He is not to be locked in a room and constantly told to shut up. There are much more constructive ways to deal with these disturbed, self-centered energies. Unfortunately, I had to learn this the hard way—through experience.

Feeling more whole than I had been feeling for a long while, I remembered my statement in the dream, *I'll have to find another way.* There was no question as to what "the other way" would be. I had to learn to surrender more, instead of struggling so much. I had already determined to surrender to life's flow, even if I couldn't understand where it was taking me. I had to do the same thing inwardly. I needed to learn to just relax inside instead of fighting with my mind so much.

Just because the voice talks doesn't mean I have to listen to it or let it affect the direction of my life. It has nothing to do with me—I can just relax regardless of what it's saying. I was back to the basics: I am the one who notices the voice talking.

I came out of silence for the rest of my stay at the community. I don't mean I talked a lot, because I didn't. I was just social enough to where people felt comfortable talking to me. I met some of the long-time residents and listened to stories of their own journeys. Despite the changes I was going through, I didn't change my meditation and yoga sessions. They were not the problem; I was the problem. I had built a mental concept of absolute discipline that was actually holding me back. In my meditations, I had been achieving heights by pushing down on the lower energies. But that was just a form of suppression. I had to learn to channel those energies upward instead of pushing them away from me. It took some time, but I eventually began to realize the true purpose of yoga. Done properly, yoga is the science of channeling all energies upward until they merge together at the highest point—Oneness.

After a few weeks at the community, I started my journey home. It was a wiser, clearer person who drove back to Florida. Though the seeds had been planted and some very deep lessons had been learned, it was going to take some time for me to learn how to come to peace with myself. Meanwhile, I was looking forward to returning home to my land and to the solitude of my beautiful house in the woods.

19.

Acceptance, Acceptance, and More Acceptance

My mind remained very peaceful during my drive across the country. But I faced a serious challenge to my vow of acceptance the moment I arrived home. As I drove through the woods onto the interior field, instead of the characteristic silence, I heard the buzz of a circular saw. I then saw Sandy and my friend Bob Gould donned in carpentry aprons and climbing on a structure they were building on my land. It was one of those rub-your-eyes-in-disbelief moments.

I asked what was going on. Sandy cheerfully informed me that she was building a house, and Bob Gould had agreed to help her. I don't recall the demeanor of my voice, but I reminded her that this was my land on which she was building her house. Again, very cheerfully, Sandy replied that she was laying no claims to the house, and it would be mine when she decided to leave. She obviously had worked it all out in her head and had no problem with it. I decided I'd better go home and meditate a bit before responding.

Imagine what that voice in my head was saying: *Oh my God! How dare she make a decision like that without even asking me? I don't want another house on my land. I don't want anyone else staying out here, so why would I want another house? How in the world does someone make a decision to build a house on someone else's property without ever asking them?* On and on it went, but by then I was well trained to just calmly observe all these thoughts being created by the preference-driven mind. After all, if I had wanted another house on the property that voice would be saying, *What a miracle! God stepped in and started building me a second house without my having to do a single thing.* To me, it didn't matter what that voice was saying. I knew to the core of my being that I was not going to give him the time of day, not to mention the run of my life. If I had a choice between using this real-life situation to get my way or to free myself from being bound to my way, I would choose freedom every time. That was the essence of my experiment with life: if it's down to a matter of preference—life wins. So I went back up the hill, strapped on an apron, and helped them build Sandy's house.

It felt good to be building again. This time around I was not a greenhorn—I was a carpenter. The difference is amazing between the first time you do something and the next. I felt like I knew what I was doing, and that gave me a sense of confidence and inner strength. I wasn't working on the house for Sandy, or for myself; the flow of life had placed me in this situation. It was during the building of Sandy's cabin that I first started the ritual of offering my work up to the invisible force that was guiding me. I was not in charge, yet life continued to unfold as if it knew just what it was doing. I would serve that force. Call it what you want—God, Christ, Spirit. These were no longer just names of something to believe in. The events that were pulling me through life were tangible and real to me. Inwardly, I began to offer everything I did up to the Universal Force. All I wanted was to return home to that beautiful place deep inside of me. If following the invisible hand of life would take me there, so be it.

Sandy's house was very simple. It was similar to what I had thought we were going to build for my place. Her twelve-by-sixteen-foot cabin had no electricity, no plumbing, no inside siding, and the window openings were covered with only screens and some plastic. It only took about six weeks to build and cost almost nothing, but she loved it. I smile now when I look back at my initial resistance. I could never have imagined how many important life experiences of mine would end up being tied to that cabin.

Meanwhile, summer was over and the time to start my classes at Santa Fe was rapidly approaching. I had been true to my commitment of not allowing a single thought to enter my mind about what I was going to teach. How would I ever know what life was capable of doing if I was always in control? I walked into my first class at Santa Fe completely open to whatever would unfold. As the students filed in, I simply quieted my mind and asked myself, *Do you have something worthwhile to teach these students?* In my heart I knew that I had a wealth of knowledge that would be both interesting and beneficial to their lives. So I took a breath, stood up, and just started speaking. I couldn't have known it at the time, but that exact moment was laying the groundwork for the next phase of my spiritual journey: becoming a teacher.

The words just flowed out. There was no prior thinking involved. The first session laid out the road map of what we were going to do in the class, just as though a curriculum had been decided beforehand. It was similar to when I was writing that economics paper in my van in the woods. Except this time, I was watching a continuous stream of inspiration turning into a powerful lecture. I was not doing any of this—I was just aware of it.

As the semester progressed, this kept happening class after class. I was amazed by what was being taught in these classes. It was as though all the knowledge from my schooling, plus all that I had learned through introspective meditation and the relentless watching of the voice, was being woven together into a cohesive whole. The premise of the course was centered on the possibility that one underlying truth exists in the universe, and all of man's knowledge was just looking at this truth from different perspectives. The exploration of that premise would involve physics, biology, psychology, and religion. What was the possibility that they were all saying the same thing? I had never thought about things in this way before. In fact, I had spent my time learning to not make thoughts a pastime. How could each class come out so perfectly without my doing it? Nonetheless, the presentation was unfolding on a class-by-class basis before my eyes.

The success of the classes was overwhelming. I would start the semester with twenty students in the room, and by the end the count had doubled. I remember one class where I literally had trouble entering the classroom. Twenty students were registered and another forty or so were either sitting in class or listening from the hallway. People would just keep bringing their friends. I was still into being quiet and didn't want all this to become a distraction to my practices. So I tried to isolate myself by coming to school just before class, leaving right afterward, and not attending any faculty meetings or school functions. It didn't matter. This was the '70s, and I was teaching Universal Thought in the midst of the consciousness revolution. Over time, students and their friends began to show up for the Sunday meditations at my place.

As if that were not enough, those classes at Santa Fe laid the groundwork for another very spiritual flow of events. This time it was regarding, of all things, my doctoral dissertation. I had been telling Dr. Goffman that my life had taken me far from the field of economics, and I had no intention of writing a dissertation. Nonetheless, one day he made me promise, as a personal favor to him, that I would turn in something, anything, for him to read. I had great love and respect for Dr. Goffman, and I saw it as an act of surrender to acquiesce to his wishes. That very night, I sat down on the floor of my house, lit my kerosene lamp, and asked myself if I had something to write that was worth such an enormous undertaking. It only took a moment to realize that I did have something very important to write, and I would love for Dr. Goffman to read it. It seems that life had just given me the perfect opportunity to write about that voice in your head and the oneness behind all of science and religion—just as I had been teaching in my classes at Santa Fe.

With that as the topic, I was filled with inspiration. Though I knew it wouldn't be accepted as an economics dissertation, I put my heart and soul into my writing. As it turned out, the finished document had an unexpected destiny of its own. A professor on my doctoral committee had a publisher contact me, and within a year, my dissertation was published under the title *The Search for Truth*. Thirty-five years later, that book still sells copies every month on Amazon—a fitting tribute to the acts of surrender that brought it into this world.

What is important from all this is that if I had listened to my own mind, none of this would have happened. By following the flow of life, instead of my own preferences, I was now a carpenter, a teacher, and a published author. Inwardly, I had grown as well. The sharp line I had drawn between spiritual and nonspiritual had begun to fade. The energy I experienced while teaching my classes at Santa Fe was the same energy I was dealing with in my yoga and meditations. In meditation, that energy would flow upward and lift me away from my everyday self. When I stood in front of a class, the very same energy would explode into a passionate, heartfelt lecture. Not only did I begin to see all this as the flow of spiritual energy, but I also began to see that there was no difference between coming to class to teach and driving home to do my meditative practices. I was teaching those classes because an amazing flow of events had put me there. I was driving home because an amazing flow of events had put me there. Neither of these destinations was decided by me. They were the result of my letting go of myself. Little by little, the fabric of my life was composed of the results of my surrender. I was becoming surrounded by a life that had been built for me, not by me. In my wildest dreams, however, I could never have imagined where this was going to lead me.

20

The Most Important
Thing I Was Ever
Asked to Do

The summer of 1973 ushered in some very interesting changes where I lived. Through no effort of my own, many of the five-acre lots around my property were being purchased by folks drawn to a back-to-nature lifestyle. Unsurprisingly, many of these people were into some form of meditation and yoga. I was still holding on to my self-concept of a meditator wanting solitude in the woods, so I had little interaction with my new neighbors. I must admit, however, that my afternoon walks became more interesting as various rough-sawn cabins began to spring up in the woods around me.

A man named Bob Tilchin purchased the property directly behind my house. I had not known him before, but he was into yoga and Sufism and was a very gentle soul. He hired my friend Bob Gould to help him build his house, so it all felt like family. One day Bob Tilchin came to me and asked me to do him a favor. He was pen pals with an inmate named Jerry at Union Correctional Institution (UCI), a maximum-security prison about forty miles north of Gainesville. Bob had promised to visit this inmate once in a while but now had to go out of town. He asked me if I would visit Jerry while he was gone. This was a very strange request for me. I had no prior experience in this area, and I was still very protective of my attempts to live a solitary life. As the voice of my thoughts said *No,* the voice of my lips said "Yes." I had no idea what it would be like to go into a maximum-security prison to meet a total stranger, but I was about to find out.

I drove up to the prison one Saturday morning and met Jerry, a young black man, in the designated visiting area. We spent a few hours together discussing topics similar to what I had been teaching in my classes. He seemed genuinely interested, and he was a very intelligent young man. He had been doing meditation for some time, so we spent a while meditating together. Jerry expressed his appreciation for the visit and asked me to come back. I had noticed that other than Bob Tilchin and me, no one else was on Jerry's approved visitors list. Our meditation together had been amazingly deep, and I felt overwhelmed by peace when I left the prison. Somehow, being in that setting had touched something very deep within me. Before I was even out of the gate, I was looking forward to coming back.

When I returned to see Jerry for the second time, he had a surprise for me. He had so enjoyed our visit and our meditation together that he had created a list of five or six other inmates who wanted to meet for group meditation. I contacted the authorities and found out that such a group meeting would only be possible as a religious service. Jerry considered himself a Buddhist, and I had done Zen Buddhist meditation, so I started what was probably the first Buddhist group in the history of a North Florida prison. We met in the chapel every other Saturday morning, and the whole scene was quite surreal for someone with my background. When I arrived at the prison, I would pass through the main gate that was surrounded by double coils of razor wire. I would then pass through two more gates before I was searched and patted down. Shortly thereafter, a call would come across the loud speakers in the various cell blocks, "BUDDHIST." From a very quiet place deep inside myself, I watched that voice in my head say, *How in the world did I get here?*

The group grew over the years, and when Jerry was transferred to Florida State Prison, I also did a group there. It may have been acts of surrender that originally put me into those prison groups, but once

I was there it was my heart and soul. Whenever I would go into the prisons, I would feel a powerful increase in the spiritual energy flow within me. And my meditations were much deeper when I sat with the inmates than when I sat for hours at home by myself. I didn't understand what was happening, but I looked forward to every visit as an experience of spiritual upliftment.

I ran the groups pretty much like the classes at Santa Fe. I did not plan any sessions; I just let the energy give the talks. The men were able to relate immediately to the notion of the talkative voice in their head. They were very receptive to learning how to quiet that voice and deal with the inner patterns of anger, fear, and strong drives. The inmates' deep-seated sincerity about their spiritual growth made those prison groups one of the most rewarding experiences of my life. A single request from my neighbor Bob Tilchin, to which I had initial resistance, grew into more than thirty years of working with the incarcerated. The men in my group became a part of my extended family, and they continue to live in a place deep in my heart.

It was the summer of 1973, and in the most unlikely of places, my heart center was learning to open. I was being taught how to serve. This is not something I would have come up with on my own. My whole being thought my path to self-realization was about meditation. Fortunately, life knew better, and she was starting to guide me away from myself through service to others.

From Solitude

to Service

21.

The Call of a
Living Master

Summers are brutal in Florida, even in the woods. My house had no air-conditioning, and with a solid wall of glass facing west, it did not exactly have passive solar design. I still had a few months left before my classes at Santa Fe started again in mid-September, so I took a drive back out to northern California for a visit. Before returning home, I got wind that Shelly, my ex-wife, was living at some sort of yoga center in the San Francisco area. I managed to get the number and gave her a call. I had not seen her for a few years, and it fascinated me that I had gotten so deeply into yoga and evidently so had she.

I drove down to Piedmont and found where Shelly was staying. It was great to see her again, and my heart felt very open. She began to show me around the beautiful house that served as a meditation center for a small number of residents. We went upstairs to see the meditation room, and once again, life caught me completely by surprise. Scattered around the room were photographs of a yoga master they called Baba. I had never heard of him, but there was no reason I would have. I had been living in the woods of north-central Florida for a few years by then, and he lived in India. The pictures of that holy man were mesmerizing. I could not take my eyes off them. The energy flow inside of me welled up to the point between my eyebrows, and a tremendous peace came over my whole being. I asked if I could meditate there for a while. Shelly nodded and went about her business.

I meditated in that room for hours with shimmering energy coursing throughout my body. The whole room seemed to be filled with energy. Something was going on that I didn't understand. I only knew that I was being drawn into deep meditation without my normal struggle. I stayed in the room for a very long time, and when I finally came out, it was time to bid Shelly good-bye. That was certainly not the visit I had imagined. What had started out as a very personal trip, life had managed to turn into a powerful spiritual experience. If that had been all that transpired from the visit, it would have been fantastic. But it was only just the beginning.

I returned home in early September to find someone I didn't know staying at Sandy's house. Evidently, Sandy had gone on a trip and allowed a friend, Rama Malone, to stay at her place. Rama was very outgoing and vivacious. She was filled with excitement and immediately drew me into her world. The first time I went up to meet her, she invited me into the cabin to show me what she had done with the place. Very enthusiastically, she beckoned me up to the loft. I climbed the rough-sawn ladder, and when my head cleared the opening, what I saw almost knocked me back downstairs. The entire loft area was covered with pictures of the same yoga master I had just encountered at Shelly's place.

Now, I believe in coincidences, but this was twice in a row on opposite sides of the continent. In 1973, there simply were not that many people in America who knew of this holy man in India. It felt like he was following me. Rama immediately started telling me that Baba Muktananda was planning to come to America next year in the spring, and I should invite him to Gainesville. At first I thought we were having a fanciful conversation, until I realized she was dead serious. I took a deep breath and tried to reason with her. I reminded her that I lived alone in the woods, and I'd gone out of my way for years to not attract people. How could I be in a position to write to India and invite a highly respected yoga master to a small town in north-central Florida? There was no reasoning with her. She insisted that I write a letter to India, on Santa Fe Community College letterhead, and invite Baba to stop in Gainesville on his way from Atlanta to Miami.

I thought it was a crazy idea. My mind kept telling me that there was no way Baba would ever come here. I actually felt embarrassed to write the letter and send it off to India. But what choice did I have? I could either listen to my resistant mind, or recognize that life had brought me in contact with this great yogi, given me a deep experience sitting before his picture, and then stuck an impassioned devotee onto my own land to force me to invite him to Gainesville. Ultimately, I surrendered and mailed the letter.

Some months later I received a response telling me that someone would come to my place to discuss the possibility of a Gainesville visit. When he arrived out here, I was surprised to be meeting a very professionally dressed young man. Apparently, he was just as surprised to be meeting a hippie-type character living alone in the woods. You could tell that he wasn't all that impressed. He began to explain to me what it would take to host a weeklong visit from Baba and his entourage. They would need facilities for his staff of up to twenty people, a room large enough for fifty to a hundred people for daily sessions during the week, and a weekend retreat site that could house up to a few hundred people. He was very skeptical about my ability to arrange everything, and who could blame him. I was a part-time teacher at a community college earning $350 a month—not exactly the credentials they were looking for.

In the end, he told me I was welcome to see what I could arrange, and they would get back to me. It certainly didn't sound promising, but at least I didn't get a definitive no. Before he left, I asked him an important question: If his group was trying to get people interested in Baba, how exactly did they promote him on his world tour? I didn't think an Indian saint who spoke no English would attract that many people. All he told me was that Baba was a very powerful *Siddha* master and people would want to meet him. I didn't understand what that meant, but I figured I'd find out later.

A few months went by, and we were given a tentative date for when Baba might pass through Gainesville: January 18, 1975. The excitement about a possible visit by a world-renowned yoga master only served to accelerate the energy around my classes and the Sunday services. Each week things grew until I was forced to build a small addition onto my house to fit more people. With the publication of my book, *The Search for Truth,* in spring of 1974, the energy was fanned even more.

Rama and Sandy had both come and gone by the spring of that year, and Sandy's house sat empty until a young woman named Donna Wagner moved in. Donna was finishing her degree at the university when she started sitting in on my Santa Fe classes. Though just a few years older than the other students, Donna was more centered and mature. She had a very deep understanding of what I was teaching, and she came to most of my classes and all the Sunday services. For about a year before she moved in, it seemed like time and again we kept bumping into each other in town. These chance meetings happened so often that I began to wonder what was going on.

Donna started to help organize the Sunday group after Sandy left. She would often stay in Sandy's house on Saturday nights to help set up for and greet the people on Sunday mornings. Eventually, she just stopped going home. If I had known then that she was moving out of a nice condominium her parents had purchased for her, and into this tiny cabin in the woods with no plumbing or electricity, I might not have been so quick to let her move in. If I had known then that we were destined to fall in love, get married, and have a beautiful daughter together—given my mind-set at the time, I definitely would not have let her move in. It would take a few more years of learning to surrender before I would be capable of dropping my spiritual self-concept enough to accept the special relationships that life had in store for me.

22.

Shaktipat

We had so many things to take care of if we were going to host a visit from Baba. None of us had done anything like this before, so we had to learn things as we went along. First, we found a summer camp in the Ocala National Forest that could easily handle a large weekend retreat during its off-season. Next, we put the word out that we needed a very large house for Baba's twenty-person staff and the weekday meditation sessions. As a college town, Gainesville is not known for its large mansions, but someone contacted me and offered us the perfect house for the entire month of January. Things were definitely falling into place.

The weekend retreat was going to be the clincher. If we couldn't get enough people signed up, Baba would never come. Donna and I had to make hundreds of individual phone calls and send mailings all over the state to attract enough people. It took real surrender for me to hook up a phone at my house and use that as the contact number on all flyers and phone messages. We were passionate about getting the word out, and we had a tremendous response from all over the state.

For years I had thought that a spiritual life was about spending every day in silence and solitude. I was now running around getting all this work done. Yet somehow I felt more open and more connected to the energy flow than ever before. I kept my morning and evening meditations, but the hours in between were devoted to my classes and bringing Baba to Gainesville. I had surrendered just enough to where the flow of life was no longer something I chose to give in to—the flow had taken over my life. It had gone from subtly guiding me to running me. My mind kept telling me that after this was over I would go back to my solitary lifestyle. As usual, my mind was wrong.

Before Baba came to Gainesville, we received an invitation to attend his December retreat just outside of Atlanta. I was anxious to meet him, plus it seemed like a good idea to know what to expect when he came to Gainesville the next month. About six of us packed into my van, and we made the trip north. When we arrived at the retreat site, we were ushered into a large hall with fifty to sixty other people. So began four of the most intense days of my life.

I remember the first meditation session with Baba. We were told he would walk around among us while we were meditating. It was so dark in the room that I couldn't see anything, yet at some point I felt a strong presence behind me. It got stronger and stronger until I realized that Baba was standing right beside me. He touched the point between my eyebrows, exactly where I always felt the energy flow. He then moved on.

We had two of these meditation sessions each day. Each time I could definitely feel strong energy as Baba walked around behind me, but that was about it. It was hard to sit in that room all day. I would try to meditate just to get some privacy, but I was unable to get inside myself. Instead of my meditations getting deeper, I was locked out altogether. That was pretty much how I felt all the time—closed down. I was too spacey to think, my body hurt, and that voice in my head was driving me crazy. I was determined to sit it out, but I couldn't wait until it was over.

It went on like that until the final day, and I was very confused to say the least. On the final morning, I decided perhaps I wasn't being open enough in how I was relating to Baba. I had come to pay my respects to a great spiritual teacher, but he wasn't my teacher— Yogananda was my teacher. I decided that for this last day I would even let go of that concept and just surrender completely to the experience in front of me.

While the program was going on at the front of the hall, I sat in my seat and started to do Baba's mantra. I repeated *Om Namah Shivaya* over and over again. Before I knew it, I was very deep in meditation. All outer sounds had ceased, as had my mental chatter. I was in a place I had never been before, deep inside my heart. I felt like my heart was a giant cave that was protecting me and loving me. I was completely entranced and at peace.

It soon became time for the evening meditation session where Baba walked around tapping people. I found myself being pulled back into that very quiet place within my heart. While I was meditating, I felt Baba walk up behind me. The power emanating from him was very strong. Even though my eyes were closed and I was facing forward, I could feel the energy of his hand reaching out toward my head. The moment the palm of his hand reached above the crown of my head, what felt like ten thousand volts of electricity jumped from the base of my spine to meet his hand. It happened as fast as a bolt of lightning. In an instant, I was no longer in my body. Me, the one who lives in here, the one who looks out through the eyes and hears through the ears, the center of conscious awareness that notices the thoughts and emotions—I was no longer sitting inside doing those things. I was in a state of absolute panic trying to hold on with all my might to my connection with the body. The upward rush of that much energy had dislodged me from where I normally sat within myself. I was experiencing tornado force winds trying to blow me out of my body, and I was struggling to hold on for dear life.

No matter how hard I tried, I could not pull myself back into the body. It was one of those survival moments when pure fear opens you up to superhuman strength. It didn't matter—I could not even begin to pull against that force. I have no idea how long the experience lasted, but when Baba felt I'd had enough, he simply rubbed his hand across my back. The moment his hand physically touched my midback—everything stopped. I immediately fell back into my body and began to get somewhat oriented. The first thing I noticed was my heart—it wasn't beating; it was fluttering like the wings of a hummingbird. My first thought was, *This is not good. Hearts don't last very long like this.* The moment that thought formed in my mind, Baba reached in front of me and rubbed his hand over my heart. Instantly, my heart began beating normally.

I was stunned by the experience and the power of this man. Who was he? How could he possibly have such control over my energy and my metabolic functions? I felt so humbled to be in his presence. I have never felt so completely unburdened in my life. What had I been doing—fasting, meditating, and struggling with myself for so many years? With a single touch, this man could bring about such transformation. At that moment I understood what was meant by a *Siddha* master. Baba did not belong in this world; he was from somewhere else altogether.

23

Gainesville Hosts a Guru

We were invited to accompany Baba's group back to where they were staying in Atlanta. As I drove from the retreat, I contemplated what had happened the previous day. One of Baba's people told me that the experience was called *shaktipat*, a special blessing by a *Siddha* master in which a very powerful spiritual energy is awakened within. When we arrived at the mansion in Atlanta where Baba was staying, his staff just assumed that I would now see Baba as my teacher. They told me it was common that one would be drawn to a living master. What did I know? All this was way out of my league.

I went outside to be alone. There was no question about what had happened the previous day or about the flow of events that had brought it all together. I remembered my commitment to surrender to life's flow, even if I didn't understand what was happening. I walked down the hill to the garage area where there were no people. I was very confused, but I prepared to thank Yogananda for his guidance. I closed my eyes to go into the quiet place within where I always felt a connection to him. I inwardly looked upward as if to say thank you, and suddenly the whole space above me opened up into a limitless expanse. It felt as if a veil had been lifted from between my consciousness and that which was beyond me. I immediately felt oneness with all that I had been looking for. It was the most powerful and revealing experience I ever had. It only lasted a few moments, but I came back with an echo in my being saying, *Just exactly who do you think you are saying good-bye to?* I felt Yogananda's presence all around me and permeating me from within. From that moment forward, I never questioned my connection to him.

When I rejoined Donna and my friends at the main house, they were making preparations to return home. As we headed back to Gainesville, we were all inspired about hosting Baba in just a few days. When he finally arrived, I couldn't believe how much attention he drew. Every place we went it was standing room only. And though Baba was not a young man when he came through Gainesville, every day and night he would give lectures wherever people would invite him. I was doing my prison work at the time, and his staff told me that Baba would definitely want to go to the prison. We got it set up, and one afternoon we accompanied Baba into the maximum-security facility. The inmates loved him, and when Baba left, he instructed his staff to continue visiting prisons. To this day, they trace all their worldwide prison work back to Baba's visit to Union Correctional Institution outside of Gainesville.

The weekend retreat ended up being the largest retreat up to that point on Baba's world tour. I drove down to the camp a few days early to see if Baba's staff needed anything. While I was there I noticed a dormitory building that had a VIP sign on the front door. Apparently, these were private rooms assigned to special guests. One of the names posted on a door caught my attention: R. Friedland. Shelly's maiden name was Friedland, and her brother's name was Ronnie. My mind said, *No way,* and I just kept walking.

I was stunned to see Ronnie at the retreat. We had not seen each other for years. It didn't matter—we were like brothers. How could we possibly have gone our separate ways and ended up at the same place? We were so different. I was living the simple life in Gainesville, and he was a big-time attorney in Chicago. I prided myself on having no belongings, and he had a Ferrari, a Harley-Davidson motorcycle, and a private plane. Ronnie lived in a top-floor penthouse at Chicago's famous Twin Towers Marina, and he decorated the circular walls of his living room with pictures of Napoleon. What in the world was he doing here at this spiritual retreat hanging out with a holy man from India?

Shelly had introduced Ronnie to Baba, and apparently it was love at first sight. I spent a lot of time with Ronnie at the retreat, and he even invited me to accompany him when he took Baba and a few of his staff to Disney World. It was obvious that Ronnie had something very special going with Baba. I found out just how special when a few months later I received my first mailing from the new organization Baba formed in America. It was signed by the foundation's first president, Ron Friedland. My thoughts drifted back to that first awakening I'd had while sitting on that couch with Ronnie years earlier. My life had completely changed—apparently so had his.

24

The Temple Is Built

I wish I could say that things went back to normal after Baba left, but they didn't. In fact, it wasn't until after he left that I began to see the real effect that meeting him had on my life. Baba was like a wind that blew into town and permanently changed the direction of my life from one of solitude to one of service. And that was a good thing because Gainesville's spiritual community had been invigorated. Forty to fifty people were coming out to my place for Sunday services, half of whom had to sit outside on my decks. Plus, more and more people were sitting in on my classes at Santa Fe, especially once my second book, *Three Essays on Universal Law,* was published. My answering machine was getting calls from all over the state praising the retreat and asking when the next one would be. This was a timely question since at the retreat I was approached by a university professor who wanted us to host a retreat for his teacher, Ma Yogashakti, a lady saint from India known as Mataji.

The number of tasks life was giving me was out of control, but I was surrendering to it. My morning and evening meditations were my refuge. Throughout the day I took every opportunity to quiet myself and center within. Every time I got into or out of my car, I would slow down my breath and visualize Earth spinning through outer space. Before opening a door, any door, I would remember that I was walking through a door on this tiny planet in the vast emptiness of space. Fortunately, the energy flowing up to the point between my eyebrows helped me keep the focus of my attention there. I slowly began to realize that this life of constant service was the "other way" referred to in the dream I had. On my new path to awakening, life was no longer an obstacle to my growth. Life was now the battlefield on which I was to remain conscious enough to willingly permit my old self to be stripped away. But let it be clear, I still had plenty of resistance left in me that had to be overcome.

I kept getting pushed in the direction of hosting a retreat for Mataji. I had never heard of her, and I really didn't want to do it. But I surrendered, and once again life had something unexpected in store for me. A few days prior to the retreat, Mataji and I were taking a walk on my land when she suddenly stopped and looked into the woods. She stood there motionless for a few moments and then said in a quiet voice, "Mickey, this is a very holy piece of land. Someday there will be a great temple here, and many people will come." I clearly remember the voice in my head saying, *Over my dead body!* Yet, within six months, a temple would be sitting in that exact spot in the woods.

It was as though Mataji had been sent here to begin the process of turning my place of solitude into a spiritual center. More than once at the retreat she mentioned that there was going to be a great temple on Mickey's land. I cringed every time she said it. The following Sunday after services, someone announced that if we wanted to build a temple, we needed to start raising some money. A few people made small donations, and others offered me their labor and some materials. I really didn't want another building on my land, but it seemed everyone else did. Fortunately, by now I had become pretty experienced at ignoring what "I" wanted and, instead, following the flow of life.

That same Sunday, I walked down to my house, took out a piece of paper, and began designing the new temple. In just a few hours, I had a floor plan and a rough elevation of the building. I wanted to make the roof of the temple the main design feature, so I met with my friend Bob Gould, and we decided to give the temple a butterfly roof. A butterfly roof challenges conventional roof design because it's low in the middle and slopes up on both sides. From the inside, the temple's exposed-beam ceiling would be a unique and dynamic structure that looked like giant wings opening up toward the sky.

I designed the temple to allow about three times the sitting area afforded by my house. The very next day, I found the best spot on the land to locate the building and began clearing the site. It was, of course, exactly where Mataji had been staring when she pronounced that a "great temple will be built." I had estimated that materials for the temple would cost about eight thousand dollars. Labor was not a problem; we would just do all the work ourselves. But the people who came out to my place on Sundays didn't exactly have deep pockets. I had no idea where the money would come from.

The money just kept showing up the moment we needed it. Sometimes I didn't even know where it came from. The closest we came to being stopped was on a day when only one or two boards were left in the materials pile. My coworkers were ribbing me that it had finally happened—we were out of materials, and I would have to send them home. I told them that as long as there was a single board left, we were not done. We broke for lunch, and I went out to check the mail. Sitting in my mailbox was an envelope with two thousand dollars in cash. There was no name, and to this day I have no idea who put that money there. Things like that just kept happening, again and again. The amazing part was not just that the money kept showing up exactly when we needed it—it kept showing up in exactly the amounts we needed to go to the next step.

That is how the temple got built. It took about three months, then suddenly one day it was done. In September 1975, we held our first Sunday service in the new temple. People brought gifts of spiritual items that had meaning to them. A professor of religion brought a beautiful wood statuette of the Buddha. Another person brought a picture of Jesus for the altar, and I went down to my house and got my favorite picture of Yogananda, which had been sitting in my meditation space since I moved in.

Little by little, the items in the temple began to represent all religions, all saints, and all masters. As its roof rafters stretched up toward the sky, the temple also belonged to those whose religion was the reality of the Infinite. This temple sat on the planet Earth, a tiny ball spinning through the vast darkness of empty space. It spun around one star, of which there were billions in our galaxy alone. This temple was universal in its embrace of all the religions, and it was universal in its embrace of the universe itself. Thus it came to be called—Temple of the Universe.

The Temple of the Universe, with its dynamic butterfly roof, under construction, 1975.

25.

Opening the Heart Chakra

There was no putting the genie back in the bottle. Between the retreats, my books, my classes, and the Temple, we were on the map for people into yoga and the New Age movement. Running retreats for visiting spiritual teachers must have been what we were supposed to be doing because I kept getting requests, one after the other. Before the Temple was even complete, I had accepted responsibility for sponsoring another retreat for a spiritual teacher I had never heard of. As fate would have it, this teacher would end up being an important part of my life for years to come.

Amrit Desai was different from our other Indian visitors. He had lived in America for many years and had a large spiritual community up north. When he arrived at the Temple, I was surprised by how many people he attracted. The first night's gathering completely filled the Temple. After the program, which was very powerful, I found myself intrigued by Amrit's energy. I wanted to understand how so much energy could emanate from a person, especially since Amrit never even touched anyone. I then got pretty brazen. I figured he was a guest in our house, and a proper host would make sure that his guest was taken care of. I took a deep breath and walked into the guest room where Amrit had gone. He seemed to be meditating, so I quietly walked over and sat down next to him.

The moment I sat down, it was as though I could feel a semblance of what he was feeling. The energy flow inside me increased significantly, and I felt as though I had been dropped into an ocean of love. It was a deeply spiritual experience. We sat quietly for a while, and then he turned toward me and said, "I never do this anymore." He placed his right hand over my forehead, and I immediately felt a gentle flow of warm energy passing into my body. The flow was overwhelmingly powerful, and I became completely transfixed by the beauty of the experience. I could feel the energy building up within me and rising toward my heart. It filled my heart fuller and fuller until it burst open. I have never felt so much love in my entire life. I was completely overcome by the flow of energy starting from his hand, coursing through me, and then pouring out of the burst-open heart area. By the time Amrit removed his hand from my forehead, I was so filled with energy that I couldn't move. When I finally tried to stand up, it felt like a powerful magnetic field was attached to my body. I couldn't speak, so I didn't say a word to Amrit as I left the room.

Over the next few hours, the force field of energy surrounding my body was slowly drawn back into my heart. I avoided touching anyone because I noticed that contact seemed to ground the energy. Eventually, the outer field subsided, but not the inner flow. A channel had been opened in my heart, and a warm flow of energy kept passing through it. Just as the powerful meditation in the forest had left a flow of energy always rising to the point between my eyebrows, so the touch of Amrit's hand left a beautiful flow of energy always passing through my heart. It has been more than thirty-five years now and neither of these energy flows has ever subsided, not even for a moment. Sometimes they are stronger than other times, but they are always there. The simple touch of Amrit's hand had permanently opened my heart *chakra*.

As the universe would have it, Amrit's visit had another lasting influence on our lives. Just as Mataji had brought up the topic of a temple on my property, so Amrit encouraged people to come out to the Temple regularly for daily meditations. He never discussed this with me beforehand, and I just about died when he kept pushing people to do their daily practices at my place. This experiment in surrender was stealing my life. My morning and evening meditation periods were sacrosanct to me. I had no interest in sharing those periods with others. Amrit not only invited others out, he specifically told me that I should support them in their daily practices by meeting with them each morning and evening. Once again, life was not asking me—it was telling me.

I reminded myself that I had tried as hard as I could to break free of myself for years. I had resolved to find another way that did not have my mind as my spiritual adviser. Sharing my meditation time with others was just the next step in the unfolding dance with life. By now I was seeing a pattern. I was continuously being pushed headfirst into a life that centered on serving other people's spiritual growth instead of my own. I never consciously would have decided to do this. I was not wise enough or selfless enough to make such a decision. It was simply the fact that I had resolved to surrender to life, and this is where life was taking me.

When I was building the Temple, my mind kept telling me that it was a stupid thing to do. Coming out to my place on Sundays was just a fad that would fade away. Soon I would end up with an empty building on my property. I ignored all that negative chatter and just kept building. I reflected back on those thoughts once the Temple was being used every day, morning and evening. Now, I reflect back on them even more with the gift of hindsight. Every single Sunday for over thirty-five years, seventy to eighty people have found their way out to this temple in the middle of the woods. We never advertised and don't even have signs that show the way. Still people come, every week. Likewise, people have always shown up for my Monday and Thursday night talks, as well as for the rest of our morning and evening programs. It seems as though life knew exactly what it was doing, and as usual, my mind knew nothing.

26

Get Thee to an Ashram

March of 1976 marked the official formation of Temple of the Universe as a federally recognized nonprofit organization. To this organization, I signed over the ownership of my ten acres along with the Temple building, Donna's cabin, and my house. I was back to owning nothing but my van, and that was exactly the way I wanted it. I was almost thirty years old, and my financial life was very simple. I was earning less than $5,000 a year, I had no assets or debt, and there was nothing I longed for that money could buy. I liked being free from having to deal with finances. I wanted to quiet my mind, and keeping life simple was certainly a help. Amrit's group had offered the Temple 15 percent of the retreat profits, but I refused. We had not made anything from the other retreats, and there was something very beautiful about keeping it that way.

Amrit's visit was by no means the end of the retreats or of visiting teachers. Our address and phone number were now everywhere in the New Age community, and whoever was touring Florida tended to drop by for at least an evening lecture.[1] We ran annual retreats for Mataji and Amrit for many years and ran two very large retreats for Ram Dass, an immensely popular American spiritual teacher.

By now, Donna had become an integral part of my life. There was way too much work for one person to do, and she perfectly filled in

---

1 An example of such a visit was when a Zen teacher was passing through in the 1980s and asked to stop by for dinner. When I arrived, I was stunned to find Philip Kapleau, the author of *Three Pillars of Zen,* sitting at the table. The flow of life had magically given me the opportunity to thank him for the great help he had provided on my spiritual journey.

the gaps. Aside from preparing for Sunday services, she handled all the kitchen responsibilities for the retreats and even allowed me to move my phone up to her house so that she could handle the Temple calls. Donna and I ended up spending more and more time together, and a tremendous love flowed between us. The events of the preceding few years had not just been happening to me; they had just as much happened to her. That created a powerful bond between us, and in the summer of 1976 we decided to make it official and get married.

The thought of getting married again was not completely comfortable to me. I was still holding on to the concept that all this external activity in my life was temporary. I would soon be allowed to return to my days spent in meditation and yoga. This relationship with Donna was forcing me to surrender my concepts of what I thought should be going on. I had not been looking for love or marriage, but the powerful flow of life managed to bless me with both. Fortunately for me, Donna was very spiritually oriented in her own right. We each enjoyed our quiet time, and we had no intention of giving up our separate houses once we were married.

As if things were not changing fast enough, returning home from our July wedding trip to Amrit's revealed that another phase of our lives had already begun. It seems that once we had started holding evening and early morning services in the Temple, periodically someone would spend the night in the Temple's guest room. When we returned, we found that not only had someone stayed there the whole time we were gone, but a very sincere seeker named Radha Kautz had stayed in my house. As in the case of Sandy a few years earlier, no one had actually asked to move in; they just ended up living here. Donna and I had just returned from visiting a spiritual community—now it appeared we were supposed to live in one.

The fact is, I never even dreamed of starting a spiritual center. It all just happened by surrendering to the flow of life. Though there was at least some internal resistance each step of the way, I just kept letting go. Sharing my place of solitude certainly wasn't what I thought

I wanted, but that's because I didn't understand that serving others is much higher than serving yourself. Nowadays, almost forty years later, people sometimes ask me how the Temple community got started. What am I to tell them? I know perfectly well that I didn't do it. The best I can say is that I let go of myself and allowed what was meant to be—to be.

. . . .

The Business

of Surrender

27

A Company Is Born

I n December of 1976, the next event took place that epitomized the essence of my surrender experiment. Just as the direction of my life had changed by my reluctantly surrendering to tutoring Alan Robertson, teaching at Santa Fe, and inviting Baba to Gainesville, so I was about to again be asked to do something that seemed askew from my chosen path but ended up perfectly aligned with my life's destiny.

I had just come home from teaching at Santa Fe and was taking a quiet walk in the woods. I turned down the narrow path that led in front of the Temple, and what I saw made me stop in my tracks. A sheriff's patrol car was parked right in front of the Temple building. It was quite intimidating, as was the fully uniformed deputy standing by the car. In all these years, I had never seen law enforcement out here. The deputy called out to me, "Are you in charge here?" The voice in my head was frantically trying to figure out what was going on. *Why is a deputy here? Is something wrong? Did he look in the Temple and see all the strange religious icons? This is north-central Florida; am I in trouble?*

Despite all this internal noise, I managed to utter a fairly normal sounding, "Yes, sir, I am in charge. How may I help you?" Pointing to the Temple, Deputy Knowles asked me if I had built the building. When I told him that I had, he asked if I would consider building an addition onto his house. It seemed he loved the rustic cedar look of the Temple and was impressed with the quality of the carpentry. He had been looking for a builder to enclose and remodel his garage into living space.

I was dumbfounded. I had never even thought of such a thing. Sure, I had built a few buildings on my own land, but I had never thought of building for someone else—not to mention someone official, like a sheriff's deputy. I stood there for a moment as two contrasting responses went on inside my head. First, the voice was saying, *No way, I don't want to do this. I'm busy. I have my job at Santa Fe, and I'm not a builder, anyway.* Second, there was a quiet, peaceful sense of awareness that didn't have to say a word. It simply knew that my vow of surrender to life required me to see where this would lead. I took a breath, looked up at the officer, and said, "Yes, I would be glad to help out with your project." There—it was said, just like the other times. Now I would get to see what magical rabbit hole this new act of surrender would lead me down.

Deputy Knowles was the perfect person for my first construction job. He knew just what he wanted, and he allowed me to do the job on a cost-plus basis. That was essential since I was in no position to give him a firm bid or pay for the materials myself. Given what I was accustomed to earning in those days, I'm sure I did the job for far less than anyone else would have. I would need an assistant, and Radha, one of our new Temple residents, volunteered. She was on her Christmas break from the university, and she assured me that she could handle a hammer and carry her load. We strapped on aprons and drove into town to do some building.

That job, completely unasked for and unexpected, became the start of my construction company, Built with Love. Officer Knowles was so pleased with the job that he passed the word around. In no time at all, I was doing numerous home improvement jobs for officers and staff at the Alachua County Sheriff's Department. I still had my ponytail, and always worked in sandals, but no one seemed to mind. Radha could only help part-time, so I did some of the jobs by myself. I put in fireplaces, closed in a few garages, and added a number of porches. I treated each job as if the universe itself had given it to me— because it had. Just as the retreats had taught me to serve, so doing home improvement work for all these wonderful people became part of my spiritual practices. I was given the opportunity to bring joy into the lives of people I didn't even know. I really liked that aspect of the work, and I would have gladly done the jobs for free. But that was not what was happening. I was going to have to learn to deal with accepting money and running a business. Life was making me let go of my spiritual self-concept, and I was staying very conscious about not replacing it with yet another one. I simply put my whole heart into whatever I was doing. There was no difference between teaching my classes at Santa Fe, meeting with people for morning and evening services at the Temple, running spiritual retreats, or doing a construction job. All these tasks had one thing in common: they had all been given to me by surrendering to life's incomprehensible flow.

28

The Master Builder

When something is meant to be, it's fascinating watching it unfold, one event after the other. To begin with, I had to deal with the money that was coming in. These were all small home improvement jobs, but they were bringing in much more money than I was used to dealing with. It turned out that Radha had some experience in bookkeeping. During summer vacations, she used to help out in the bookkeeping department at the Florida Farm Bureau, where her father was president. I'd never seen anyone use an adding machine as fast as her fingers could fly across the keys. I had minored in accounting in college, so together we set up the company's books. I imagine my CPA brother-in-law, Harvey, must have been surprised when I called him for advice on setting up a business. He filed the paperwork to incorporate Built with Love and offered to look over the books and handle the annual tax returns. This had to be the smallest business in the world that had a CPA. As usual, it all seemed like overkill to me, until the next unlikely event took place.

Not long after the start of Built with Love, we were meeting on the field one Sunday after services. It was our tradition to get together in a big circle for community announcements before sharing tea and cookies. After announcements, a man came up to me and said he had heard I was doing some building. I concurred, and he asked me if I could use a builder license. Any permits needed so far had been pulled by the home owner, but it would be good to have a contractor license in case anything bigger showed up. I told him I would be interested, and he informed me that he had a builder license that I could use. He had the look of a devoted hippie, and I hadn't pictured him as a licensed contractor. I asked him how he came about having a license. He told me that a few years earlier there had been a period of dispute between the county and state licensing agencies. During that time, anyone could fill out the paperwork and be issued a contractor license. He had done just that, and now he had an active license. It seemed too good to be true. I called the county the next day and asked about the license number he had given me. I was informed that the license was active and in good standing, and I was free to work out any arrangement whereby Built with Love could utilize the license.

Just in case the flow of life hadn't already been impressive enough, I was now a licensed contractor. And it was a good thing, because I soon had a very special building project to do on Temple property. It seems Donna's twelve-by-sixteen-foot cabin was not going to be big enough to house both her and the child she was expecting. I would not have had the wherewithal to build an addition onto her house just a few months earlier. The perfection of the Universal Flow I had been surrendering to had taken care of the problem before I even knew there was one. We hadn't changed our lifestyle, so the funds that Built with Love had been earning all got plowed back into the Temple's property. I knocked out an entire side of Donna's cabin and built an addition that included room for a crib and a proper bathroom.

Our daughter, Durga Devi, was born in August 1977. Amrit, Mataji, and many others sent her traditional gifts of blessings for health, prosperity, and spirituality. She was born into what had become a spiritual community. It was going to be very interesting to see how she would grow up.

You would think that it was time to settle in and digest all the changes that had taken place in our lives. I had always lived within my means, even when earning $350 a month as a part-time teacher at Santa Fe. Now, Built with Love was earning me a few thousand a month on top of my Santa Fe salary. There was certainly no need for more income—at least that's what I thought. It had become a pattern of mine to think, or wish, that an energy flow was complete when, in fact, it had just begun. It's a good thing I was following the energy and not leading it, because the Universal Plan was always much more expansive than my mind could imagine.

Just before Durga was born, I received a call from a commercial outfit wanting to convert an ABC liquor store in Gainesville into a clothing store. I had never done a commercial job, but it was permitted under Built with Love's license. By then I had a crew doing most of the work, and I was driving around in a pickup truck playing contractor. I got the job, but before I could even begin, the fun started. The woman in charge of getting the store open called me and insisted that I come over immediately for a meeting. When I arrived, she explained that they had changed their plans and needed some extra work done. I offered to work up a change in price, but she got very irate and said she didn't care about the cost; she wanted it done right away. As her energy got intense, I began to quiet my breath and focus on my mantra. Even back then I used my work in the world as an opportunity to let go of myself and remain calmly centered. I politely, though somewhat kiddingly, asked if she wanted me to immediately drive to where my crew was working, pull them off the job, and have them do the extra work right away. I knew I was in trouble when she said, "Yes, that is exactly what I want." I told her that it was going to be an expensive proposition, and she told me in no uncertain terms that she was on a very tight schedule and throughout the job would be demanding a lot of me, but her company was willing to pay whatever it took to get it done. I assured her that I would do the best I could to help them out.

Throughout the job, she kept changing things and wanting everything done yesterday. But she also kept throwing money at the job to be sure I was properly motivated. I got the work done in close to half the time originally allotted, in spite of all the changes. With all the bonuses, change orders, and overtime charges, I walked away from that job in just four weeks with a profit of around $35,000. I remember that amount because it was way beyond the few thousand a month I had been earning and because of what happened next. I received a call from a neighbor who owned one of the five-acre lots that adjoined our land. She had been building two very rustic cabins on her property but had now decided to move. She informed me that she would accept $37,000 if I could come up with the up-front cash she wanted.

To say I was humbled by the fact that I had just earned almost exactly the same amount of money on that very strange job would be an understatement. I saw a synchronous flow that I would never forget for the rest of my life. Was this part of some Universal Plan that the Temple expand beyond the original ten acres? I had no interest in such an expansion; I had never even thought of it. But the money was there, and it was obvious what it was intended for. None of this had anything to do with me—I was just the middleman, the caretaker. I didn't feel like the money was mine. I had never asked for it or gone out of my way to get a single job for Built with Love. The jobs just came by word of mouth, one after the other, and I served them to the best of my ability. All I had to do now was simply step aside and allow the money from that very strange job to be used to purchase our neighbor's property in the name of the Temple.

29.

Community Banking

Not even a year had passed since Radha and I had finished Deputy Knowles's garage enclosure. Built with Love had grown so much that I was running two crews, and Radha was a full-time office manager/bookkeeper. Not only were we getting more and more work, but the jobs were becoming larger and larger. In September 1977, right after the clothing store job, the inevitable happened—a young couple asked me to build them a house.

Up to that point, Built with Love had been doing remodel work, and job financing was always handled by the home owner. The building of a house, however, would require a construction loan between the company and a bank. I had no assets in my name; I had signed everything over to the Temple. Any profits Built with Love was making were also being donated to the Temple. So neither the company nor I had the balance sheet necessary to obtain a first-time construction loan. I simply took the attitude that if we were meant to build houses, something would work out.

I put together a portfolio for Built with Love that included some references from jobs we had done, as well as our nine-month financial history. We hadn't even earned a hundred thousand dollars yet, so to show that I had experience in building houses, I listed the buildings I had constructed on my land. I dropped the portfolio off at a number of banks along with loan applications. When it came time for a follow-up appointment, I went from bank to bank only to receive rejection after rejection. Built with Love simply did not meet the profile necessary for a first-time construction loan.

Before giving up, I played a game with life. I agreed to follow up with just one more bank before taking it as a sign that home building was not in our future. I remember sitting in the lobby of one of the nicer banks in downtown Gainesville. I had been waiting a long time for a loan officer, but people kept being moved in front of me. It was rather disheartening, but I used the time to focus on letting go of whatever the voice was saying about the situation. That is one thing I had noticed: running the business was putting me into very different situations than I had experienced living alone in the woods. I found this very helpful to my spiritual growth. By watching different parts of my psyche get stimulated, I could learn to let them go. Without realizing it, I had become conscious enough to use sitting in a bank preparing for the inevitable loan rejection as an opportunity to fall behind whatever the voice was saying. If the whole purpose of my surrender to life was to get rid of myself, it was working out quite well.

Finally, the receptionist who had been putting every customer in front of me asked me to follow her. But she wasn't leading me to the group of loan officers in the open lobby area; she was taking me to one of the offices that overlooked the lobby. As she knocked on the door, I noticed the nameplate: Jim Owens—Branch President. I was kind of shocked but not nearly as shocked as by what happened next. I was invited into the office, and the president took his place behind the desk. He proceeded to tell me that though my application did not meet the normal standards set by the loan committee, he personally felt that a community bank should try to support community businesses. It seems Jim Owens had taken such an interest in my application that he had driven out to my land and looked in the windows of my house and the Temple building. He had then personally gone to the loan committee and hand carried my application through. He was here today to tell me that the construction loan request for $20,000 had been approved, but his neck was on the line, and I had better not let him down.

What do I say to this man? Who are these people, anyway—Alan Robertson, Rama Malone, Deputy Knowles? They're like messengers from God sent to tell me what I'm supposed to be doing with my life:

teach at Santa Fe, invite Baba to Gainesville, start Built with Love, go forth and build houses. All I could do was thank him and assure him that I would rather die than let him down.

The young couple was overjoyed, and we built them a beautiful little house. Moreover, Built with Love was now in the position to start building larger, custom homes. I felt so honored to have met a man like Jim Owens. I never thought that the president of a bank would go so far out of his way for a total stranger—especially one who lived in a spiritual community. I obviously had a lot to learn.

If I had thought this was the end of my story with Jim Owens, I would have been very wrong. A decade later, after I had experienced significant business success, the hand of life brought us back together again under the most unlikely of circumstances. I was working late one night at Donna's and decided to take a break. There was nothing on TV, so I drove in to a new video store I had noticed on the north side of Gainesville. It is worth noting that I hardly ever went into town at night. The store was empty except for someone behind the checkout counter. While I was browsing the movies in the back of the store, I couldn't help overhearing the conversation the clerk was having on the phone. He was telling someone that he had gone into a bank for a working capital loan, but it seemed banks were not going to lend to a small video store. The man looked vaguely familiar to me, but I just couldn't place him. When I went to check out, it hit me: the man behind the counter was Jim Owens.

Jim recognized me, and we caught up on the past ten years since we had last seen each other. He told me he had left banking and was now trying his hand as an entrepreneur with his own business. I apologetically told him I couldn't help overhearing his conversation about needing a loan. Mindful of what he had done for me years earlier, I asked if perhaps I could help. He looked very surprised by the offer but eventually disclosed that he was looking for a loan of about $20,000 to cover cash flow while he upgraded the store. That was pretty much the exact amount he had provided for me ten years earlier when our roles were reversed. I couldn't believe this was happening. What was the probability of these events, including my being in that store right after the bank had rejected his loan request and exactly at the time of that phone conversation? It was as though after ten years I was sent there to repay Jim's act of kindness. Needless to say, I was honored to make him that loan.

30.

The Ever-Expanding
Temple of the Universe

By the spring of 1978, Built with Love was building fine custom homes and doing large residential remodels. Around that time, I stopped teaching at Santa Fe. The college invited me to stay, but only on a full-time basis, and I would've had to use a standard sociology textbook for all my classes. It was not as though a decision had to be made; life had already given me a full-time job. The transition to Built with Love had already taken place by then. I experienced none of the mental resistance that had been present during my previous periods of change. As natural as a snake sheds its skin, so this transition in my life naturally took place.

Not too long after I left Santa Fe, I was hired to build a beautiful house for Tom Jenkins, a professional golfer on the PGA tour. As it turned out, the Jenkinses purchased a piece of property just down the road from the Temple. Only one lot lay between our interior field and that land. To me it was like another miracle—I got to build my nicest custom home within walking distance of where I lived. And if I thought that was special, I wonder what I would have thought if I had known that someday we would end up owning that house, and it would provide the perfect home for some Temple residents.

This raises a very interesting topic: the expansion of the Temple of the Universe. We had six or seven people living on Temple property by the end of 1978. We were charging rent for anyone living here, and though it wasn't much, at least no one was coming for a free ride. Built with Love taught us how to run a small business properly, and Radha ran the Temple's affairs in the same professional manner.

As fate would have it, the person who moved into our only cabin with a kitchen loved cooking vegetarian meals for dinner. It didn't take long before all of us started showing up at that house as regular dinner guests. We also got together there for holiday gatherings and birthday parties. That was pretty much as communal as we got. The people who lived at the Temple were expected to keep morning and evening services and to pay their rent—not so difficult. They were also expected to try their best to not get caught up in the incessant chatter of the personal mind—much more difficult.

It seemed as though Built with Love kept earning just enough money to allow us to purchase bordering properties as they came up for sale. I made that a game with life: if a neighboring property came up for sale and we had the funds available to purchase it, the Temple would buy it. It was then fascinating to sit back and watch how just the right people would show up to occupy those houses.

There are some amazing stories of how people ended up at the Temple, and these stories had a profound effect on my willingness to surrender to life's flow. It was as though people were handpicked to show up at just the right time in their spiritual growth—and ours. Perhaps no story is more stunning than that of a student who ended up living at the Temple for many years. I remember that I first met her when I was teaching at Santa Fe one winter toward the end of my tenure at the college. I had entered one of my classes, and the students were complaining about how the overheated room was making them sleepy. I went to a window, opened it up, and started waving in fresh air. Shortly thereafter, a new student entered the room and found herself a seat. I often had unregistered students sit in my classes, so I thought nothing of it. I also thought nothing of it when this same student started attending meditation services at the Temple. She was very sincere in her spiritual practices and eventually moved into one of the houses on Temple property. It was not until years later that she related to me how she had wanted to come to my class for a long time, but she had been too shy. She actually became teary-eyed as she told me how appreciative she was that I had seen her procrastinating on the walkway that cold winter day and opened the window to wave her in. I was stunned to hear what she thought had happened that day. When I related my side of the story, she realized it was actually life's hand that had beckoned her to rise above her fears and come into the class.

Things like that just kept happening. I became deeply committed to serving the unfolding of that force. In fact, if you had asked me toward the end of 1978, I would have told you that I had surrendered my entire life to the Universal Flow, and it had taken over every moment. It taught me how to keep regular spiritual practices while working in the world and how to support others to do the same. It taught me how to build and run a successful business that would support the ever-expanding spiritual work. It taught me how to serve others by sponsoring statewide retreats for leading spiritual figures and by providing a home for what grew to a dozen or so very special and sincere seekers. I saw this work as something that could continue to grow in a linear fashion. I would never have guessed that I had seen nothing yet. It would have been beyond my comprehension that everything I had been taught so far was just the foundation for what was coming next. No one could have guessed that all that had transpired during those early stages of my surrender experiment was just the launching of a multistaged rocket headed for the stars.

31.

Metamorphosis
of a Creature

Before moving on to the tremendous growth of the 1980s, I should share another aspect of my life that was teaching me a great deal about surrender—my prison work. No matter how busy I got, every other Saturday morning I spent my time in the prison. Once Radha finished school, she began joining me on these visits. Radha also took care of the increasing correspondence with the inmates and brought in spiritually oriented books they requested. If I had to, I would have rearranged my life to not miss any one of those visits.

It is difficult to explain how sincere those men locked up in a maximum-security prison became about their inner freedom. The walls could hold their bodies, but nothing could imprison their souls—except their own minds. They saw this at a very deep level. I taught them meditation and how to do a little yoga. But mostly what we discussed was letting go of oneself. They learned to watch that voice in their head, and they learned how to not listen to all the garbage it says. After my talk, we would have group sharing sessions. Sometimes one of the men would relate an incident that had happened during the week where that voice had told him to do something stupid. He spoke about that brief moment of awareness wherein he got to choose whether to listen or just let it go. Invariably, while telling the story the inmate would start laughing about how in the past he would have just immediately expressed that destructive behavior. This time, he just let it go. My heart would melt listening to them share with one another how to do this—how to let go of yourself. No words can express how honored and grateful I was that life had serendipitously put me in those sessions.

Most of my group were in for life, but periodically some of them would get shipped off to another institution. The ones who stayed at Union Correctional Institution for a long time formed deep bonds and encouraged one another in the spiritual life. Often one person in the group got the teachings so deeply that he became a leader for the others. I will recount the story of one such unlikely person because of the insights into surrender that the story portrays.

It was back in 1975 when I first met David. My group was meeting upstairs in the chapel at Union Correctional Institution when a very large man walked up front and sat down close to me. He was the size of an NFL football player, not fat, just big. After my talk, he came up to me and said, "Hey, my name's Creature, and I'm an Outlaw." I had heard of the Outlaws; they were a motorcycle gang like the Hells Angels. I got up, stuck out my hand, and said, "Hi, I'm Mickey." That was my first encounter with a guy named Creature.

The name on Creature's shirt read: DAVID CLARK. He came to every one of my classes from that day forward. Most of my group was either black or Hispanic, and David stood out as a white southerner. It intrigued me as to what would keep a person with his history in this group. Little by little, I saw that he was very sincere in wanting to improve himself and grow spiritually. He started to ask for a number of books. He began with Yogananda's *Autobiography of a Yogi*. A few visits later, I noticed that Creature was carrying a picture of Yogananda around with him. I didn't know what to make of this very sincere and intelligent person who was serving multiple life sentences for what he had done as one of the leaders of one of the most violent motorcycle gangs in the country. I will tell you that I felt tremendous love for him and was deeply honored that life had brought us together at this important stage of his growth.

David would generally approach me after class and ask some very deep questions indicative of someone who had been meditating a lot. In fact, I could tell from his interaction with others in the group that David had been organizing meditation sessions for the men in his cell block. This went on for years. David became a leader who was obviously friends with, and respected by, the rest of the group.

One day, David approached me and said something had happened that was going to affect his ability to come to the group. Authorities had apparently uncovered the bodies of some rival gang members from many years earlier, and David and a few other Outlaws were going to be charged. He didn't seem disturbed by this turn of events. In fact, he told me that he saw it as a way of working off some of his past karma. He had done bad things in the past, and he wanted the opportunity to work them through. I was humbled by how completely surrendered and at peace David was with the situation.

While awaiting trial, David was placed in confinement in the high-security lockup cells of a building called the Rock. The Rock housed the original cell blocks at UCI, which dated back to 1925. The living conditions were so atrocious in the Rock that it was finally torn down in 1999 under court order. I was not allowed to see David while he was in lockup, but he wrote and told me that he had been spending hours a day in meditation and chanting.

Once when Amrit was scheduled to come down for one of his annual retreats, David wrote us about how much it would mean to him to meet a great yogi like Amrit. David knew that given his condition, it would never happen. But you could feel the sincerity of his devotion radiate from the letter. I sent the letter to Amrit and asked if he was willing to visit David if I could arrange it. Amrit had never been in a prison before, but he was very moved by the letter and David's whole story. Amrit's simple response was, "How could I not?"

I used every connection I had at the prison. I had become very close with the chaplain over the years, and the warden was familiar with me because of donations we had made. Each year after the start of Built with Love, we would donate thousands of dollars to enhance the chapel and help the chaplain serve the needs of the inmates.

Ultimately, I received permission for a visit between Amrit and David. The conditions were very strict. David could not come out; Amrit and I would have to go into the lockup area of the Rock to meet him. I will never forget that day. Amrit wore a saintly off-white gown that flowed when he walked. When we made it through the main gates into the prison, we remained silent because Amrit wanted to feel what it was like to live in there. I could never succeed in describing what it was like to walk into the Rock. Each wing we walked by was just a solid row of barred cells on one side facing a stone wall on the other. There was not one drop of color anywhere. But we were not going to one of those cells. We were led right past those wings to a dark area where there were no windows. This was the lockup area of the Rock. We were led to a dimly lit cell that must have been used for meetings. It was a one-man cell with a filthy toilet sitting bare in the middle of the room. There was a small, broken table with three chairs and nothing else. Amrit and I took our seats at the wobbly table while a number of guards stood around.

After a short while, David was led into the cell. He was shackled hands and feet, but he looked beautiful to me. I was so glad to see him again. We hugged, and I introduced him to Amrit. We all took our seats at the table with David sitting opposite Amrit. We sat there for a long time with David's head facing downward. The energy in the room felt like the Temple after Amrit had finished chanting mantras. It was so strong that you could hardly think. Not a word was spoken until Amrit asked David what he was feeling. David lifted his head to speak, and that was the first time I could see his face. Tears were pouring down his cheeks, and his face was aglow with a gentle light. In a whisper of a voice he said, "I guess I'm feeling how much love you have for me, because I'm completely overwhelmed with love." Those were the only words spoken that day. We sat in silence for a while longer, and the guards took David back to confinement. Amrit and I were escorted out of that dark hole, past the wings of cell blocks, and out of the Rock. We were left to find our own way back to the front gates.

As my eyes acclimated to the sunlight, I was overcome by a single thought. On this earth, there are many different places where people live. Some are high places and some are low places. That hole where David was living in solitary lockup, a veritable prison within a prison, had to be one of the lowest places on earth for a human being to end up. You couldn't go much lower. Yet the sincerity of his spiritual practices had just attracted one of the higher beings on the planet into that dark hole.

I never got to ask David what he experienced that day, but he was glowing when he left. I remembered what I had experienced the night Amrit put his hand on my forehead. A deep peace came over me as I realized that my dear friend David would get to keep that overwhelming experience of love for the rest of his life.[2]

---

2 For those interested, at trial David threw himself at the mercy of the court. Based upon his prison behavior record, he was sentenced to time to be served concurrent with his existing sentence. In essence, David got to work out his past without one day added to his sentence. David was transferred from UCI shortly after this ordeal. I got word that he had earned a "trusted-inmate" status at his new facility and was working in the chapel. I lost touch with David after that.

Something Priceless

Is Born

32

From the Personal Self to
the Personal Computer

I t was in the fall of 1978 when, without a clue, an event took place that changed everything once again. It is so inspiring to look back and see how a handful of moments in your life define your destiny. What if life had not presented those moments to you, or if you had interacted with them differently? Over time, everything would be different.

I thought I knew what was being asked of me by then: run Built with Love to the best of my ability, and use the funds to support the beautiful work being done through the Temple. As usual, I was wrong, very wrong. What life had in store for me was much grander in both size and scope. How could I ever have imagined that I would end up running a $300-million-a-year computer software company, with twenty-three hundred people reporting to me, all without leaving the woods of Alachua or putting aside my spiritual pursuits? How could the flow of life's events pull that off, especially since I had never even touched a computer in my life and was totally content with my finances? As I sit here today, if I were forced to answer that question, I would utter the word *surrender*. My experiment with surrender had taught me to always be present in the current moment and do my best to not allow my personal preferences to make decisions for me. Instead, I allowed the reality of life to determine where I was going. It had certainly led me on a fantastic journey up to that point, and it was about to do something phenomenal with the next thirty years of my life. If you would like to know how these phenomenal events unfolded in a perfectly choreographed sequence, I would be very honored to share the story with you.

It all began one uneventful day when I walked into a neighborhood Radio Shack store to pick up something for Built with Love. On my way out, I noticed what appeared to be a plastic typewriter keyboard attached to a twelve-inch TV screen. The two items had a TRS-80 COM-PUTER sign displayed above them. As fate would have it, I had just encountered one of the first personal computers on the market. Being a curious person, I walked up to the display and punched a few keys. As if by magic, the keys I touched appeared on the monitor above. I had never experienced that in my life. I had only taken an introduction to computers course in college, and everything we did was on punch cards. We were never allowed to go near the workstations that were actually connected to the computer itself.

I was absolutely fascinated by this Radio Shack device. It opened something inside of me that can only be described as love at first sight. I stood there playing with the machine for a long time. I marveled at typing in simple and complex math computations and seeing the results pop up. I finally tore myself away from the display, but I knew I'd be back. From the first time I touched that machine, there was an inner calling from the deepest recesses of my being. I had no choice but to surrender to that calling. When I returned to the Radio Shack store a few days later to lay out $600 for their best computer, I really had no idea what I was going to do with the thing when I got it home. I just knew I was meant to have it.

My first computer was a Radio Shack TRS-80 Model I with just 16k of memory, a twelve-inch monitor, and a standard cassette recorder for storage. That was all that was available at the time. It came with a simple user's manual for the BASIC programming language, and that was about it—you were pretty much on your own.

When I got the computer home, I buried myself in learning the programming commands and seeing what they could do. For some reason, everything was so natural to me. It wasn't like I was learning something new; it was like I was remembering something I had always known. My mind became very quiet the moment I sat down at the machine. It was very much like entering meditation. The energy would rise up and focus beautifully at the point between my eyebrows, and a peace would come over me. Apparently, I was meant to be working with this computer. I didn't question it—I just continued to surrender to what was happening.

Before the computer showed up, I already had two full-time jobs: Temple of the Universe and Built with Love. To find time for my new computer, I began to go back to work after evening services. I would often work into the wee hours of the morning, getting only three or four hours of sleep before rising for morning services. I was so passionately inspired while working with the computer that I didn't get tired. It was clear to me even then that something very special was going on.

I played around writing some programs just to get a feel for what the thing could do. Within a few weeks I decided that I was ready to write a real program. The first task I gave myself was to write a computerized accounting system for Built with Love. I had to teach myself everything. The salespeople at the Radio Shack store knew nothing about programming, and I didn't know anyone else to talk to. I just used trial and error as my teacher.

Once I had completed Built with Love's accounting system, things progressed very rapidly with my programming. I had made friends with the manager of the Radio Shack store, and whenever I went in I would show him printouts of the work I had done. He was impressed with what I had gotten the machine to do and began asking if he could refer some clients to me. To my surprise, he ended up sending me people who wanted programs written. All of a sudden, I had a new business. As unbelievable as it seems, this humble beginning was the birth of what was to become Personalized Programming, a nationwide, multimillion-dollar software company.

As with everything else in my life since I decided to follow the flow,

Personalized Programming just started itself. There were no meetings, business plans, or venture capitalists. Just as with the Temple of the Universe and Built with Love, I simply accepted the challenge of serving the energy that came my way. I never left the woods; all of this came to me unasked for and unwanted. Fortunately, I really loved helping people. I didn't care if they were coming to me to learn how to still that voice in their head, to build them a house, or to write them a program—it was all the same to me. I passionately loved programming, and I loved getting to use that talent to help people.

At first the jobs were small, and I had no idea what to charge for them. I wrote a grading program for a University of Florida professor for $300. I was such a perfectionist that I just kept making it better and better before I was willing to give it to him. From the very beginning of my programming career, my heart demanded that every line of code had to be the absolute best I could do. It didn't matter what I was being paid; everything had to be perfect.

During 1979, I began spending more and more time sitting in a room programming by myself. When the manager at Radio Shack asked if he could refer his customers to me, I had no idea what to expect. I started getting calls from Radio Shack stores all around Gainesville and from stores as far away as Jacksonville. Soon I was getting more requests than I could handle. Being schooled in economics and understanding the law of supply and demand, I began raising my prices. It didn't help; the jobs just kept on coming. Around that time, I began noticing that every job seemed perfectly sequenced to advance me to the next level in my programming career. Though I was sitting in the woods working alone, let there be no doubt about it, life was turning me into a professional programmer.

It didn't take long for me to realize that writing custom software took a lot of time, and I was better off selling available software to satisfy my client's needs. I became a dealer of one of the top accounting software packages sold by a company called Systems Plus in California. I don't recall how I selected that particular software, but as I look back now, it must have been an inspired decision—I ended up having some serious destiny with that company.

By late 1979, I was doing more and more work selling the accounting package and the related hardware and support. I took such good care of my clients that even Systems Plus began referring customers to me. Just as I had learned all my programming skills through the jobs that came to me, so these new jobs were teaching me how to analyze, implement, and support the computerization of various-sized businesses.

Word spread like wildfire, and the demand for my products and services kept increasing. Between references from Systems Plus, Radio Shack, and my existing clients, I started getting requests from businesses scattered across the state. But I was only one person, and I was very committed to attending morning and evening services at the Temple. To avoid overnight business trips, I just let those opportunities go and fully surrendered to putting my spiritual practices first. I would have gone on like that, but then James showed up.

James Pierson was a very sincere seeker who had just moved into one of the houses on Temple property. As perfection would have it, James had a pilot's license. One day he overheard me discussing my inability to take on out-of-town clients, and he offered to fly me around. If we rented a small, single-engine plane for the trips, James's rates were more than reasonable. We began to do day trips to the out-of-town clients who were willing to pay a premium for my services. These tended to be upscale businesses, like a client in West Palm who brokered private jets. With life as my teacher, little by little this non-suit-wearing hippie from the woods of Alachua was learning to deal professionally with successful businesspeople. My formula for success was very simple: Do whatever is put in front of you with all your heart and soul without regard for personal results. Do the work as though it were given to you by the universe itself—because it was.

Personalized Programming was always an exciting business. Now I got to fly above the clouds in a tiny two-seater plane. I would often look out over the expansive sky and wonder, *How did I get here?* I had moved out to the woods to drop out and devote my life to my spiritual practices. I never left the woods, and I never for a moment took my life back. Now a boutique business in West Palm, one of the most affluent cities in the United States, had hired me to fly down and computerize the business. It was all beyond my comprehension. I was never even trained in any of this. I was just living in a fairy tale.

33.

The Birth of
The Medical Manager

Personalized Programming had grown into a successful, one-man company. In 1980, my brother-in-law, Harvey, suggested that I incorporate the business for liability purposes. I remember how unnecessary it seemed to incorporate yet another business. Still, I accepted his advice and registered Personalized Programming with the State of Florida. The State sent me a stock certificate for the business, which I stuck in my safety deposit box at the bank. The certificate had a beautiful official-looking seal on it, but it had no real value to anyone but me. Nonetheless, Personalized Programming, Inc. was now a legal corporation in the State of Florida.

I really loved the work I was doing with Personalized Programming. If anything, my passion for computers had grown stronger since that first day in Radio Shack. Each computer I installed was like a dear friend I left behind to serve my clients. I may have looked like a one-man company, but in reality I had left my workers at every one of my clients' sites. They worked for free day and night, and they never complained.

Once I started selling and supporting full system solutions for my clients, Personalized Programming began generating more than a hundred thousand dollars a year. That was a far cry from the five thousand I was earning at Santa Fe just a few years earlier. In addition, Built with Love was still earning a decent living. Through all this, I had hardly changed my lifestyle. The money the businesses were earning got donated to the Temple to support land purchases and the expenses incurred serving the community. The perfection of how everything was unfolding was enough to silence the personal mind. It was around that time when I noticed that my mental concepts separating *worldly* and *spiritual* had finally dissolved. Everything began to appear as the miraculous perfection of the flow of life.

If I'd had my way, I would have continued my life in that direction. But somehow it seems that in my experiment with surrender—I never have my way. So it was in early 1980 when I received two phone calls on the same day that would end up initiating the next stage of my phenomenal journey. The calls seemed innocent enough; they were from people looking for a medical billing system. What they wanted was the ability to do patient and insurance billing using a personal computer. I didn't have a system that could do that, but I told them I would look around and get back to them.

After some searching, I found a system through a contact I had in Miami. It was supposed to be a nationally distributed software package with successful installations. I should have checked references. I got literature and pricing on the system and got back to my prospective clients with a bid. I had no idea what I was getting into. Once I started testing the software, it didn't take long to realize that the package was absolute garbage. There was no way I was going to represent that software.

When I called my clients to give them the bad news, they each had the same response. They said they had heard that I was a very reliable programmer who had written custom software for numerous businesses. Why couldn't I write software for their medical practice business?

I remember I was sitting on the floor of my small office. The little voice in my head was going on about how it took so long to write software versus selling someone else's. Writing a patient and insurance billing system would be a much larger project than anything I had ever done. I told my clients that it could take as much as two years to finish such a system. Unfortunately, they both said they were willing to wait if they could give input along the way. I definitely didn't want to get into a programming project of that size. But though there was no definitive agreement with these clients, there was my agreement to honor life's flow. My mind became still as I realized that I really had no choice but to surrender to the situation life had put me in. It was just like all the other times I let go when I didn't want to. I took a deep breath and told both clients that I would try my best to write a billing system for their medical practices.

The moment I hung up from these phone calls, I reached over and picked up the standard insurance claim form that was lying on the floor next to me. I had obtained it earlier to see what an insurance bill looked like. I began thinking about how I was going to structure a program that would collect and store the diverse data necessary to fill out this form. Little did I know that those first thoughts were the start of a journey into the computerization of the medical industry that would span almost three decades. People have often asked me how back in 1980 I had the foresight to focus Personalized Programming on the medical industry. Now you see that the answer is simple: I didn't do a thing except serve with all my heart and soul what life brought before me. But the scope of the task I had been given this time was way beyond anything I had ever faced.

There were no meetings, or budgets, or project plans. There was just me. I immediately started to code the software that would come to be called The Medical Manager—a product that would end up revolutionizing the U.S. medical practice management industry. I know it is difficult for people to understand, but to me writing code was the same as having a conversation with another human being. I didn't have to think about what I wanted to say or how to say it. There was just a natural flow directly from the stream of my thoughts into the machine. When I was writing a program, the voice in my head would speak in the computer language I was using. I didn't think in English and then convert to the language; my primary thoughts were in the computer language to begin with. Because of this, I could just sit down at the computer and write perfectly structured code. We are back to our earlier discussions of inspiration and where it comes from. Beethoven heard music and he wrote it down. Artists have creative visions and they manifest them. I never saw The Medical Manager all at once in some grand vision. Nonetheless, every day the constant flow of inspiration let me know exactly where the program needed to go. I simply sat at the computer and wrote down the spontaneous stream of inspired thoughts in the form of code.

I wrote and wrote with a fervor and passion that was almost frightening, first the patient record, then the medical procedures that needed to be billed. Everything I did, I did to the absolute best of my ability. I was not only writing a program for these two clients; I was writing the best program I possibly could as my gift to the universe. The flow of inspiration was such that I was not allowed to cut a single corner. This commitment to detail would end up distinguishing The Medical Manager from almost all competitive medical billing systems on the market. In short, this thing wanted to be as close to perfect as possible regardless of how long it took or how unreasonable it appeared from a business perspective.

The fact is, there never really was a business perspective. I figured I could probably sell the program to some other doctors in town, but I never once thought about broader distribution. I was able to cover the cost of program development out of my own pocket because of the perfection of how events had unfolded. And I don't use the term perfection lightly. During the time I was writing the medical billing system, a subdivision opened up in the woods just one mile down the road from Temple property. Built with Love landed a number of contracts for custom houses in that subdivision, which meant I didn't have to go anywhere to handle the jobs. In addition, Personalized Programming had its existing clients. I hired a young man part-time to help me do some of the small custom programming jobs for those clients. I trained him on the old programs I had written, and I reviewed and tested his code. Without realizing it, while I thought I was training him, it was really me who was getting trained on how to manage programmers. That was a skill I would definitely need in the near future. Turns out, I was destined to manage hundreds of highly skilled software developers.

34

The Early Programmers

No person in their right mind would think that they were going to sit down and write an entire medical billing system on their own. I, however, was not in my right mind. I had accepted the project as the next task given to me by the flow of life. That was a very holy thing to me. My entire spiritual path was focused around my experiment with surrender. In order to keep my distance from the inner chatter, I still maintained my regular meditation schedule and continued my moment-to-moment practice of centering myself. Every time I sat down at the computer to work on the program, I took a breath and remembered that I was writing this as a gift to the universe. I was sitting on a tiny planet spinning through outer space, and this was the task that had been given to me. It never even occurred to me to ask for assistance.

The program was about half complete when my guardian angel sent me unasked for, but much needed, assistance. Some moments in our lives are marked by destiny. Such was the brief moment in time that occurred one fall day in 1980. I was navigating through the Sunday morning crowd on the Temple porch when a young lady approached me. I did not recognize her, and she spoke so softly that I could hardly hear her above the crowd. As a way of introducing herself, she said that she had just graduated from the University of Florida where she had taken a few programming classes. She had heard that I had been programming and wanted to work with me, even if it meant no salary to begin with. Her name was Barbara Duncan.

I certainly needed help, but I couldn't imagine how anyone could help me. I had been writing the program directly from my mind into the computer. There were no hook points where someone else could tie in. In addition, I didn't know this person, and she seemed very shy. Fortunately, I was well trained in watching these thoughts pass through my mind, rather than blindly listening to them. I simply stopped for a moment, took a breath, and recognized all this negativity as my mind's initial resistance to change. I immediately let go and surrendered to the reality of the situation: this person had sincerely offered her services, and I was certainly in need of help. I told her that because I was used to working alone, I couldn't make any promises. However, I was willing to give it a try. We set up for a meeting in a few days, and I told her that she should think about a reasonable starting salary because I wanted to compensate her.

The level of talent and competence that was hidden inside this person who just happened to show up at the Temple is beyond my comprehension. Barbara was definitely very scared and shy in the beginning. Then for the next twenty years she kept stepping forward to accept and excel at whatever was asked of her. She also started coming to all the Temple's daily services and moved in shortly after starting to work for me. Barbara was really Personalized Programming's first full-time employee, and she became a foundation block of both the company and the Temple community. It turns out that this shy young lady I met on the Temple porch that day had a brilliant mind and the heart of a warrior.

When Barbara started working for me, I was already halfway done with the program. I had never actually verbalized my thoughts to anyone, so sharing my vision for the overall system with another person helped tremendously. We made a wonderful team, and it was clear that Barbara was perfectly capable of taking my vision and running with it. This became essential once the number of programmers began to grow. In short, Barbara was a gift from God. She showed up exactly when I needed her, at a time I was not even wise enough to know that I needed her. I never looked for her; she just appeared.

In truth, it was the same with Radha. From day one she took

responsibility for all the accounting and office management functions of the businesses and the Temple. Thirty years later she is still living at the Temple and managing its affairs. It was as though these people were handpicked for the disciplined spiritual lifestyle of the Temple and were also perfectly suited for the highly skilled jobs that were being created. I saw this happen again and again as the businesses expanded. It felt like I was dancing with the perfection of the universe. I didn't fully realize it at the time, but witnessing the results of my surrender experiment was doing more to get rid of the burdensome sense of "me" than my hours of spiritual practices. I was well aware that I was not causing these events to unfold so perfectly, but I was deeply honored to watch the perfection of life unfold before my eyes.

We brought on a couple of additional programmers over the next year. By the time we were done with the first version of the software, there were four of us working full-time. We needed the additional help coding mostly because the designs Barb and I were turning out were never the simplest way to get things done—they were simply the best way. For example, one of the most interesting and important modules we wrote was the one that printed the insurance claim forms. I remember the days I spent with my clients going over their insurance billing needs. You basically had to be a rocket scientist to understand all the minute differences between how these practices were filling out the supposedly standardized forms. But they insisted that each of these differences was essential in order to get properly paid by different insurance companies.

Barb and I managed to develop a very sophisticated, template-driven system that would allow the practices themselves to specify how they wanted to fill out the forms for any particular insurance company. We were committed to developing a system that would perfectly handle a practice's insurance billing needs, and this became one of the main reasons for the rapid acceptance of the software. In a very short period of time, Medical Manager practices would be defining hundreds of different templates needed to handle the nation's insurance companies.

This provides a glimpse of the level we went to with The Medical Manager, even with the very first version. We kept bearing down and doing everything to the best of our ability. I had never in my life been involved in anything that demanded the level of perfection of that program. It was like a polished diamond by the time it was done. To me it was a living entity, and I felt tremendous respect every time I touched it. Just look at the amazing flow of life's events that created this program. I felt like it had a life of its own, and we were just here to serve it.

It was the beginning of 1982, and after two years of intense development, we started installing the program for my original two clients. Given that none of us had ever written such a comprehensive program before, the installations moved along very smoothly. I never once thought about what would happen after those sites were installed. We were completely focused on writing and delivering the absolutely best system we could because that was the task life had given us. The program's destiny after the initial installations would have to unfold completely on its own—exactly as had happened every step of the way so far.

35

Preparing for Launch

Along with the great strides the program was making, I was pleased to see events unfolding that benefited those around me, especially Barb, who was working really hard. Around this time my neighbor Bob Tilchin decided to move, and the Temple purchased his property. Barb got to move into that house, and she also got a well-deserved new office when Personalized Programming relocated its five employees into a new building on Temple grounds. I got a nicer office as well, and some very important events were destined to take place there—none more important than a destiny-filled phone call I took while sitting at my computer one day.

We had just finished our first installation of The Medical Manager, and I was finishing up the manual for the program when the phone rang. It was Systems Plus, the distributor of the accounting program we were selling. I was a very small dealer of theirs, and they didn't generally call me. I had placed a call a few days earlier to report problems with a new piece of software they were releasing.

The customer representative at Systems Plus introduced herself as Lorelei. She was very apologetic for the problems they were having. At some point in her apologies and assurances, she told me that I should remain receptive to their new software releases because they planned on being the leading company for small business software. She said they were expanding beyond general accounting and were currently looking for a top real estate package, legal package, and medical billing package.

When I heard her say medical billing package, she caught me by surprise. At first I was too embarrassed to say anything. Systems Plus was this big, Silicon Valley computer company, and I was a guy in the woods who had taught himself to program. Sure, I had spent the last two years writing our medical billing program, but it had only been installed in one small doctor's office for a few weeks. Though the voice in my head was assuring me that Systems Plus would have no interest in my little software program, I took a breath, surrendered to the moment, and informed Lorelei that I had just finished a medical billing package. She started to say something and then stopped. After a brief pause she said, "Wait a minute, my boss just walked by; let me see if he's interested." I had absolutely no idea what to think.

When Lorelei returned to the call, she told me her boss was very interested in reviewing any software that could do a medical practice's billing. She encouraged me to send in the system along with the manual I was just completing. We got off the phone, and I was stunned. What had just happened? I had never even thought about finding a software distributor. Then one of the industry's top business software distributors calls me in the middle of the woods in Alachua, Florida, and ends up asking to see my system. I found out later that when Lorelei mentioned her boss, she was referring to the president of the company, Rick Mehrlich, who had just happened to walk by her desk at that exact moment. Perhaps now you can see why I have learned to so deeply honor the flow of life.

It took me a week or two to pull everything together and ship it off to Systems Plus headquarters. There was something very surreal as I stood there offering the finished package up to the universe. I had simply been following the flow. I hadn't had any expectations, hopes, or dreams about anything. For many years now, I had just been putting one foot in front of the other serving whatever was put before me to the best of my ability. To me, I was not a computer programmer; I was a yogi living in the middle of the woods. I had bought a tiny toy computer for $600 some years earlier, and I had played around with it. I got tricked into spending two years of my life writing a medical billing package after my mind had already decided that writing software was too time-consuming. Now, without my making a single call, I was about to send something I had programmed off to the president of a successful software company out in California. How does such a thing happen—even in a fairy tale?

A few weeks later, I got a call from Systems Plus informing me that the company president wanted to fly out to Alachua to meet me face-to-face. I agreed, and in no time at all Rick Mehrlich was sitting on the couch in my office telling me that he wanted to distribute my software. He said it was about the best he had ever seen, and he could do a great job representing it in the marketplace. I enjoyed both his frankness and his positive praise, and I immediately felt comfortable working with him. It is important to understand that the way I viewed the unfolding events was that this man sitting before me had been handpicked by the Universal Force to take my child out into the world. Just as Barb had shown up out of nowhere and turned out to be the absolutely perfect person to help me, so this man might as well have manifested out of thin air and told me he had been sent to distribute the software package.

I neither contacted another distributor nor viewed any other options. I surrendered to the perfection of the flow. As Rick and I shook hands on our intent to enter into a distribution arrangement, we couldn't possibly have known that for the next few decades of our lives we would be involved in a fantastic voyage together. It should come as no surprise that Rick and Systems Plus turned out to be the absolutely perfect distributor for The Medical Manager product. Life had worked its magic once again.

Systems Plus informed me in September that the company was going to launch The Medical Manager in November at the upcoming 1982 Computer Dealers' Exhibition (COMDEX). Held in Las Vegas each year, COMDEX was the largest computer trade show in the country and the second largest in the world. Systems Plus was planning to feature the product in its huge booth, so the pressure was on to get the distribution agreement signed and to ship the finished version of the software out to California.

It turns out that the Temple had a large retreat scheduled for first of October that year for Ram Dass. That was exactly the deadline Systems Plus had given me to send them the finished version. Since I didn't get the software shipped before leaving for the retreat, Ram Dass ended up with it on his lap the entire drive down. At one point he asked me in his very no-nonsense way of speaking, "Is it any good?" I answered him by saying that I had no idea; it could be worth nothing or it could be worth a million dollars. Turns out I was off by a few zeros. I always had tremendous respect for Ram Dass, as do all of us who grew up under his aura of absolute honesty with one's self. The perfection of circumstances that had him holding that piece of software just before it launched into the world was amazing to me. Who knows how these things work? I certainly don't claim to know a thing. I watched how this software was conceived, and I saw it attract exactly what it needed to not only get written but to be a leader right out of the gate. It then magically attracted its own first-rate distributor and was now sitting on the lap of one of the most-respected New Age spiritual teachers in the world. This program had a destiny of its own, and it was about to take us all on a journey, the likes of which we never could have imagined.

Section VI

The Forces of

Natural Growth

36.

The Foundations of a

Successful Business

The launch of The Medical Manager at the Las Vegas trade show was a sight to behold. I flew out to see Systems Plus at work and to meet the company's people. I had never been to anything like that show in my life. Remember, I had been living in the woods for years. At Systems Plus's booth, THE MEDICAL MANAGER banners were plastered all over the place. It's one thing to see your kid grow up for eighteen years and then watch her honored at her high school graduation. It's quite another thing when your kid was just born a few months ago and was now center stage of a very professional production at a show the size of COMDEX. Systems Plus had one of the larger booths at the show, and everyone did a wonderful job presenting the product. The market was ripe for medical billing software, and there was tremendous interest at the booth. I marveled at seeing all the Systems Plus salespeople demonstrate the product. The Medical Manager had no warm-up period. It went from the quiet woods of Alachua to the big-time lights of Vegas without a single step in between.

There was no time to rest on our laurels. Systems Plus immediately started signing up dealers and selling the product. What followed was an avalanche of requests for new product features and customizations. Every specialty wanted something specific, and the staff of almost every practice wanted the program to do things exactly as they were used to doing them on paper. On top of all this, within a month or two of launch, Systems Plus informed me that in addition to the wonderful billing system we had written, the dealers would need appointment scheduling and other practice management features in order to continue successfully selling the product.

How were we going to do all this? None of us had any formal training or experience in medical software design. We had to figure it all out for ourselves—and we did. If you asked me how, I would tell you that my experience with meditation had shown me that there were two very distinct aspects of what we call *mind*. There was the logical, thought-driven mind that links together what we already know into complex patterns of thought in order to come up with logical solutions. Then there was the intuitive, inspiration-driven mind that can look at a problem and instantly see a creative solution. As it turned out, the years of spiritual work I had done to quiet that voice in my head had opened the door for almost constant inspiration. It seemed that the quieter the mind, the more that solutions became self-evident. This was also true for Barb. Somehow she had the ability to almost instantly tune in to the same creative solutions I had seen and then help me work out the logic. That is how The Medical Manager was designed, and it is a tribute to this process that we led the industry for many years. Our ability to rapidly design software became legendary.

In the meantime, the interest in the product was so phenomenal that we could hardly keep up. It seemed like we were being pushed to our limits in every direction. Take the example of our dealer training seminars. We held our first annual Medical Manager dealer seminar in a small guest suite at the Gainesville Hilton in spring 1983. That one room was plenty large to hold the fifteen or twenty people in attendance. Just a few years later, we were renting the entire Gainesville Hilton Hotel, including all of its two hundred rooms, conference facilities, and dining rooms. By the early 1990s, we had outgrown the Gainesville Hilton and the guest rooms of all the surrounding hotels. To find a hotel big enough to accommodate us, we had to move the dealer seminar down to Orlando.

The spiritual growth that came from keeping up with Personalized Programming was very deep. The diversity of tasks that now made up my daily life ranged from running the Temple and giving spiritual talks three times a week, to lecturing hundreds of dealer personnel on medical practice management. Despite all these outer changes, I did not become a traditional businessman. I remained a person whose spiritual path was surrendering to the flow of life and putting his entire heart and soul into what life was giving him to do. My twice-daily meditation sessions certainly helped to keep it all in perspective.

The year 1985 would turn out to be a landmark year. In only two years, Systems Plus had signed up more than a hundred dealers, and we were averaging more than a hundred and fifty new Medical Manager installations every month. Our template design for insurance billing became a huge success, and we were able to do billing to pretty much all insurance companies across the country. But before I could catch my breath, the industry was about to go through a tremendous transformation. As more and more practices computerized, it suddenly became possible to replace paper billing with electronic billing. The advantages would prove to be so enormous that an industrywide push was about to take place. As successful as we had been with our paper billing, we had no choice but to surrender to the fact that the entire health-care industry was being pushed into the age of computer-to-computer communications. Unfortunately, that was a topic we knew nothing about. The story of how we ended up leading the industry in that area is just another tribute to the perfection of life's flow.

I remember our first design meeting for electronic claims. We realized immediately that the optimal solution would be to use templates, as we had done for paper billing. But doing this for electronic claims was way beyond the capabilities of our existing template design. As far as we knew, nobody had even attempted such a solution before. The general attitude of my programming team was that it probably could not be done, and they wouldn't even know where to begin since all the different insurance companies could require very different electronic claim files.

Nonetheless, I didn't want to give up. That very same week, another one of life's miracles took place. On Sunday after services, a man introduced himself to me as a former resident at Amrit's yoga community. He wanted to know if I might have some work for him if he settled in the area. His name was Larry Horwitz, and I vaguely remembered that some people at Amrit's had told me how bright he was. I assessed his background and talents, and it dawned on me that, once again, life may have sent us the perfect person to tackle the problem at hand. Though Larry had absolutely no background in insurance billing, he got really interested in our innovative approach to electronic claims. I decided I might as well give him a try. After only a broad overview of the project, I left him pretty much on his own to see what he could come up with.

By himself, Larry studied every one of the 250 specification books from the nation's insurance companies and mapped out exactly what we would need in order to use templates to handle the entire country with one program. We implemented these changes, and The Medical Manager now had an electronic billing program with designed technology that far surpassed others in the industry. The response was phenomenal. Larry became so busy creating the templates that we had to build an entire department around him. The insurance companies ended up changing their specifications on a regular basis, and twenty-five years later, Larry Horwitz was still in charge of electronic claims for the company. How does such a person just show up by himself exactly when needed?

The Medical Manager led the industry in electronic claims. Our ability to submit claims directly to the Blue Cross Blue Shield and Medicare insurers nationwide drove the success of the product. By 1987 we were the first practice management system in the country that was able to submit claims electronically in all fifty states. In 2000, The Medical Manager was recognized for its accomplishments in computerizing the medical industry by being installed in the permanent archives of the Smithsonian Institution. The tremendous work we did in successfully converting tens of thousands of practices to electronic transactions has been preserved for generations to come. I saw all this as just another one of life's miracles.

37

The Industry Knocks
on Our Door

Personalized Programming was truly an anomaly. We were located in the middle of the woods in a small building on Temple property. None of us were sophisticated businesspeople or experienced professional programmers. We were just people who had been brought together by the energy to do a task. Normally, successful businesses have to plan their growth by developing business plans and financial budgets. In our case, our only business plan was to try to keep up with life's powerful wave that was carrying us forward. Our only budget was to hire whoever showed up who could help us. But no matter how hard we tried, it seemed that life just kept stepping things up to another level.

A perfect example of how our miraculous growth took place organically can be seen by some unexpected phone calls I received in the mid-1980s. The first was in the spring of 1985 from a woman who introduced herself as a vice president of Empire Blue Cross Blue Shield. Empire handled New York City and was one of the largest Blue Cross Blue Shield insurance providers in the country. Part of its efforts to convert medical practices in the area to electronic claims was to sell the doctors a practice management system. The company had been developing its own software but didn't feel it was competitive with The Medical Manager. I was very honored when she told me that Empire wanted to drop its system and market The Medical Manager under a private label. You certainly couldn't beat having Blue Cross

Blue Shield marketing your product to its doctors. Before I could catch my breath, I was contacted by Blue Cross Blue Shield of New Jersey with the same request. Then came South Carolina, Georgia, Arizona, Hawaii, Mississippi, Colorado, and a few others. All those Blue Cross Blue Shields ended up marketing The Medical Manager to the doctors in their states. I saw this as a living lesson in the power of surrender. For years I had been willing to let go of my personal preferences and focus on doing the absolute best I could with what life presented me. I hadn't expected anything in return, and I was very humbled to see what was unfolding.

By the 1986–88 period, Personalized Programming had about a dozen employees, most of whom were programmers. We were a tiny company, yet we were earning millions of dollars a year in royalties alone. Systems Plus had very quickly realized the enormous potential of the medical marketplace and dropped all its other products to focus exclusively on The Medical Manager. As head of Personalized Programming, it was now my job to do business with all these large corporations. I had never worked at that level before. But just as life had given me on-the-job training to become a builder and a programmer, she was now training me to be a corporate executive. I had already seen too much, however, to be a conventional executive. Even in business, I intended to continue trusting the flow of life as my ultimate adviser.

One thing I saw again and again on this ride with life was that the right person would show up at just the right time. I literally banked on that perfection, and it is amazing how it kept happening. Even our corporate attorney, Rick Karl, was into yoga and meditation. It seemed that life was surrounding me with spiritually oriented people, not only at the Temple, but also in my business.

How life managed to do this is perhaps epitomized by the following perfectly orchestrated sequence of events. It began when Systems Plus asked us to host a representative from a laboratory equipment company who wanted to meet the Medical Manager development team. It was rare that Systems Plus sent prospects out to the woods in

Alachua, but in this case there was no choice. Systems Plus staff practically begged me to wear a jacket, laced-up shoes, and have everyone on their best professional behavior. Paul Dobbins was our visitor's name, and he had an extensive background as a senior technical analyst and product manager.

I sent Rick Karl, our very presentable attorney, to pick up the gentleman from the Gainesville airport. When he returned, Rick stuck his head in my office with a grin on his face the size of the Cheshire cat's. Then, in walks our important guest. The first thing I noticed was that he had a particular piece of jewelry wrapped around his upper arm. It looked remarkably similar to the special bangle that Yogananda used to wear. As it turned out, it was. Paul Dobbins was a follower of Yogananda, had taken the lessons, and had been doing Kriya yoga for many years. You can be sure I was shocked, but imagine how he felt. He flies in from St. Louis on this important business trip to meet the president of the company that wrote the top-rated medical practice management system in the country. He walks into the president's office and sees pictures of Yogananda all over the place.

At first, there were no words between us. Paul just sat down on the couch and took in the beauty of the moment. The energy in that room was befitting the presence of a master. I couldn't keep my eyes open, and Paul was visibly overcome. After sitting in silence for a while, I asked him if he would like to see the Temple. We walked down the tree-lined road, onto the rustic dirt path, and into that holy place adorned with the pictures of great masters. Needless to say, this was not Paul's usual business trip.

Paul extended his visit through the weekend and stayed in a small ten-by-ten-foot guest room on Temple property. Come Sunday, he didn't want to leave. Paul had apparently gotten into meditation on his own, and he didn't have many people around him who were into yoga. He was overwhelmed by what was going on at the Temple and the strength of the Gainesville spiritual community. He came to me after Sunday services with the inevitable question: "May I stay and work for you?" I felt deep in my heart that Paul belonged here and that he really wanted to be part of the Temple and the business. But I didn't feel right about him just leaving the company that had sent him here, so I told him let's wait and see how things unfold.

Some months later, I received a rather panicky call from Paul. He told me that his company had suddenly been sold, and his boss and many other employees were bailing out. Paul was turning in his resignation but wanted to continue working with The Medical Manager in some manner. Life's message was perfectly clear—it was time to offer Paul a job.

Paul arrived in less than a week with some of his belongings. We allowed him to stay in that same ten-by-ten-foot guest room until he found a place of his own. Five years later, Paul was still living in that tiny room. I have no idea what he did with his belongings, but I do know that he came to morning and evening services at the Temple like clockwork.

Paul was a tremendous asset to the company, and he showed up exactly when he was needed the most. Shortly after he joined the team, we began getting contacted by the major national laboratories. They all wanted us to interface The Medical Manager to their labs. Paul was an expert in the field, and we were one of the first practice management systems to implement electronic connectivity with the major lab companies. We could never have succeeded as we did without Paul on our team. When I reflect back on how he came to us, it looks like a gift from the universe. Twenty years later, Paul still worked for the company and, to this day, lives in a home with his wife and family bordering Temple property. It appears that some things are just meant to be.

38

The Temple Keeps
Growing

Morning meditations took on a whole new meaning as the software company got larger and larger. Not only were meditation and yoga essential for continuing my inward journey, but they were essential for keeping the mind sane. So much is demanded of you when you're running an organization on which so many people rely for their livelihood. The mind needs time to quiet down and keep everything in perspective.

Leaving Temple services on a winter morning after sunrise, we often find the field covered in a mist of dew. Giant oaks, pines, and hickory trees embrace the field on three sides, and the north side opens up to that beautiful rolling pasture that slopes down to the tree-lined stream. Just standing out there with a quiet mind is heaven on Earth.

It wasn't that way one misty morning in early December 1988. When we walked out of the quietude of the Temple onto the interior field, we heard the roar of large machinery coming from the north. To our utter surprise, we saw giant bulldozers and other land-clearing equipment on our neighbor's rolling field. We didn't know what to make of it, so we walked up the hill to my original house that bordered the pasture. We located some of the workers and asked what was going on. They told us that they had purchased lumber rights to all the trees on our neighbor's property. Our neighbor to the north was a thousand-plus-acre farm owned by a couple named Wilbur and Juliet. They were wonderful people whose house was on the farthest side of their property from the Temple. The land had been in their family for a long time, and they had great respect for the property. We didn't understand what was going on, so we gave them a call.

When I was finally able to reach Wilbur, he explained that they were clearing what was left of their native forest and planting slash pines. That would provide a cash crop some fifteen to twenty years in the future. I told him I would like to talk to him about it, and I asked if he would be willing to hold off clearing the land bordering our property until we met. He was hesitant but told me to tell the foreman to give him a call. In truth, I had no idea what I would say to Wilbur when we met, but I felt a deep obligation to do what I could to protect the beautiful woods on that land.

As I drove over to Wilbur's, I focused on remaining open and receptive to the experience at hand so that I could see where life was taking it. As I look back now, I am so grateful that surrender had taught me to willingly participate in life's dance with a quiet mind and an open heart.

When I arrived at Wilbur's, there wasn't any openness to selling us the thirty-five acres that lay between our property and the stream. I explained to him that the trees on that property were beautiful, and they should be spared. He agreed with the beautiful part, but he was running a farm, and slash pines were what they had decided to plant on the entire property. Our efforts seemed futile until I offered to lease the property at whatever price would assure that he earned more than the pines would yield him. Wilbur was an astute businessman, and that caught his attention. There was risk in any crop, but no risk in a secured, long-term lease. Wilbur named a price that was significantly higher than any farmer would pay to lease unimproved property. Nonetheless, it was still worth it from our perspective of protecting the trees and pasture of that beautiful piece of land. In the end, we signed a long-term lease with Wilbur that allowed us to preserve, protect, and have use of the property to our north—the property that I had once called the Elysian Fields.

This experience only served to reinforce what I was learning from my experiment with surrender. Something that started out looking totally disastrous had ended up with a positive result. Time and again I was seeing that if I could handle the winds of the current storm, they would end up blowing in some great gift. I was beginning to view these storms as a harbinger to transformation. Perhaps change only takes place when there is sufficient reason to overcome the inertia of everyday life. Challenging situations create the force needed to bring about change. The problem is that we generally use all the stirred-up energy intended to bring about change, to resist change. I was learning to sit quietly in the midst of the howling winds and wait to see what constructive action was being asked of me.

If that were the end of the story regarding that property, I would still label it a gift from the universe. But it was far from the end. Just one week after signing that lease, another piece of land came up for sale that bordered the core of our community. Remarkably, once we made that purchase, the land we had just leased ended up running along the entire northern border of all our property, thus tying everything together.

It left me breathless to see all this unfold the way it did. I was playing a game with life, and every time life made its move, a part of my noisy mind fell away. Why was I needed? Everything was unfolding on its own much better than anything I could ever imagine—let alone do. I had said I would purchase adjoining property if it were presented to me and if we had the necessary cash. The Temple was now up to eighty-five acres, including the leased land. As we will see shortly, this leased land was destined to play a much larger role in what life had in store for us.

It was not just with the Temple property or the meteoric success of the business that miraculous events were taking place. Little things were happening on a regular basis that were so unlikely, they chipped away at the rational mind. One of these amazing events took place during a business trip to Boston in the late '80s. With so many Blue Cross Blue Shields private-labeling The Medical Manager, I had received a request from Blue Cross Blue Shield of Massachusetts to come up for a meeting. I arrived in Boston late afternoon, and I was starved. I had rushed around all morning and not eaten a thing all day. Instead of eating junk food while traveling, I figured I would get checked into the hotel and find a nice vegetarian restaurant. I didn't know Boston at all, but I had a rental car, and how hard could it be?

I got very lost trying to find the restaurant that the concierge had suggested. After close to an hour's drive, I ended up in Harvard Square. I drove around looking for a vegetarian restaurant in that area, but I couldn't find one. In a big city like Boston, I had been hoping for a high-end vegetarian meal. Now I would be perfectly happy with just brown rice and veggies. I decided to quit driving around and just order room service from the hotel—if I could find my way back. Somehow I managed to get lost again and ended up back in Harvard Square. It dawned on me that perhaps the universe was trying to tell me something, so I parked my car and got out.

This time I looked more carefully to see if there was even a small place that might have something a vegetarian could eat. I noticed there were some narrow alleys that ran between the buildings. They were not for cars, but shops lined both sides of the walkway. I headed for one of the alleys and, lo and behold, fifty feet down the alley was a small blackboard stating, "Today's Special: Brown Rice and Fresh Vegetables." I hung my head in both relief and gratitude, but I would soon find out that I hadn't seen anything yet.

The sign led to a narrow staircase that wound down to a small restaurant. It was just perfect for the mood I was in. I ordered, and a deep peace came over me as I enjoyed the great meal that life had provided me. There was one thing, however, that was disturbing my peaceful respite. From the time I entered the restaurant, the man behind the checkout counter kept staring at me. It was enough to make me a little uncomfortable. When I was done eating, instead of the waiter bringing me the bill, the man from behind the counter brought it to me. As I reached for my wallet, he asked me a question: "By any chance, are you Mickey Singer?" I was completely stunned as the unlikely sequence of events that brought me to this restaurant flashed through my mind.

What in the world was this? I didn't know this person. I responded affirmatively, and the energy between us became intensely spiritual. He said that I wouldn't remember him, but he remembered me. Back in 1972, more than sixteen years ago, he was hitchhiking through Gainesville, and I had picked him up in my VW van. He had been going through a very difficult period in his life, and he asked me about the picture of Yogananda on my dashboard. I explained to him that I was heavily into yoga and was studying the teachings of this great yoga master. When he reached Atlanta, he was walking by a bookstore and saw Yogananda's picture in the storefront window. He went in and purchased a copy of *Autobiography of a Yogi* as I had encouraged him to do. Apparently, it changed his life. He ended up meeting Baba during the world tour and was now living in a yoga center in Boston. He said he had often wondered if I had ever met Baba; then he saw a picture of us together at Disney World. It brought him great joy, and he prayed that someday he would have the opportunity to thank me in person for the important role I had played in his awakening. With that prayer now miraculously answered, he stood quietly before me with tears in his eyes and uttered, "Thank you." That said, he turned and walked away.

As I headed down the alley toward my car, I looked back at the blackboard that had lured me into this unbelievable event. I remembered that before I walked into that restaurant I thought I knew what was going on: a very interesting flow of events had brought me to my brown rice and vegetables. I was wrong. It was much bigger than that. It's always much bigger than that—for everyone. I was so glad I had decided to devote my life to learning to surrender. I didn't know what was going on, and I had reached the point of not even wanting to know. I just wanted to cease to interfere with the perfection of life. Apparently, even a business trip to Boston is fair game for a miracle.

When Dark Clouds

Become Rainbows

39

A Touch of Magic

My birth sign is Taurus, and my nature has always been to just settle in and do my work. I wasn't the type of person who was always looking for change. I enjoyed the repetition of a stable lifestyle and gradual, sustainable growth. Both the business and the Temple went through natural stages in their growth. I always thought each stage would become the steady state.

By the early 1990s, I certainly felt that we were done with our rapid growth. Personalized Programming was in phenomenal shape. We were up to twenty employees, and the bottom line was netting a few million dollars a year. I still had not changed my personal lifestyle, so I continued using the money to build up an endowment for the Temple and to support various charities. At that time, Barb was living in my house, and I was in a small guest accommodation in the building the Temple used for dinners. This building had a long wooden boardwalk stretching across a wetlands area connecting it with Personalized Programming's office. That walk was my commute to work. Those of us living at the Temple were all working hard and keeping morning and evening services together. People from the Gainesville community were coming out regularly for my Monday and Thursday night talks, and a large crowd always found their way out on Sunday mornings. Things were good, and I thought the period of crazy growth was over. Apparently, I was wrong.

To understand the next wave of growth, it is important to understand what was going on inside of me at that time. All the events that had unfolded so far in my experiment with surrender had shown me that the more I was willing to let go of the inner noise created by my personal likes and dislikes, the more I could see subtle synchronicities in what was unfolding around me. These unexpected concurrences of events were like messages from life gently nudging me in the direction she was going. I listened to these subtle nudges instead of listening to the not-so-subtle mental and emotional reactions caused by my personal preferences. This is how I practiced surrender in everyday life, and the purpose of all these stories is to share with you the perfection of the journey that unfolded.

Take the case of the Temple property. As I've already mentioned, we had no interest in owning a lot of land. Yet, over the years, the Temple would end up with an enormous amount of property, and each purchase along the way seemed to have something magical about it. Such was the case in October of 1990 when I received a call regarding a piece of property that had come up for sale in our area. The Realtor said it was eighty-five acres of combined woods and field, and it was considered one of the most beautiful pieces of land in Alachua County. I told him that I doubted we would be interested since our primary interest was in land that bordered the Temple property. He insisted on giving me a tour, and we were both very surprised when we discovered that this exquisite piece of land actually did border directly on the Temple's leased land. That was enough of a nudge for me. I put out a minimal amount of effort, and the purchase just seemed to fall into place by itself.

I considered that land a gift from the universe. It came to us completely unexpectedly, and I was speechless seeing how these properties were lining up like pieces of a jigsaw puzzle. It was just three months later when the golfer, Tom Jenkins, called to say they were going to move, and we realized that his property was practically surrounded by our new purchase. This would mean that the Temple would now own 170 acres of contiguous land. We couldn't have done better if we had bought it all as one piece of property to begin with. It was as though each piece waited until we could afford it. The perfection of what had unfolded was stunning, but we weren't done yet.

After we closed on the Jenkins property, Radha moved into that house. At the time, she mentioned to me that I should have a better place to live than that space behind the kitchen building. The room was very small and had almost no privacy because everyone kept coming in and out of the main house day and night. I told her that I was fine, and I liked waiting for the flow of life to make things happen. She challenged me by saying that the flow had given us plenty of land and sufficient money. What did I expect—that the universe would call me on the phone one day and tell me to build a house? I told her that if I was meant to have a house, something would happen that would make it perfectly clear. In the meantime, I was fine with where I was living.

It was only two weeks later when I got a call from one of our neighbors informing me that he was about to put his house up for sale. The only lot lying between his land and my original ten acres had been purchased by the Temple years earlier. This meant that his property directly bordered Temple property. Because of the conversation I had with Radha just a few weeks earlier, I paid special attention to what my neighbor had to say. He told me that he had spent many years building a very special house, and he would like to show it to me. I played it cool on the phone, but I literally got shivers up my spine realizing what was about to happen. I called Radha and told her that she should probably come along with me to see this place—just in case this turned out to be the call from the universe regarding a house for me.

As we pulled up the long winding driveway, a beautiful chalet-style home awaited us on the back side of the property. My first impression was that there was something very special about this house. It turned out that my neighbor was a boat-level carpenter. He had spent twelve years handcrafting the house like some people would build a high-end yacht or sailboat.

The house was not large, only about eighteen hundred square feet. It sat on a twelve-acre piece of land that was so well kept that it felt like a park. Once I looked around inside, I realized that I could not have designed a more perfect house for myself if I had tried. Though every bit of the house had its own special character, there was something magical about the small third story that sat above the kitchen area. As I climbed up the steep open staircase, I felt like I was going up into a tree house. But what I found was the most perfect space for a meditation room I could imagine. The top floor was a single ten-by-twelve-foot room with every inch handcrafted into an artisan's dream. All four walls were wrapped with antique leaded glass windows that had been saved from a centuries-old admiral's house in Boston when it was taken down. The result was so exquisite that standing there you felt like you had been transported back to the eighteenth century. As if that were not enough, when I looked up, I realized that the top floor was covered with a cupola. Its exposed beams came to a high peak in the center of the room, making it feel as though you were standing inside a pyramid. The space was so exquisite that the mind became quiet just being there.

Needless to say, I purchased the house and have lived there ever since. The magic of how all these properties joined together came to a crescendo with this latest purchase. My neighbor had always entered his property using his front driveway. It only took a moment of exploration to realize that the back side of the property directly bordered the field we had leased from Wilbur. Once we cut an opening in the trees behind the house, I could drive or walk to the Temple without leaving Temple property. Amazingly, this one field now seamlessly tied together all the properties we had purchased over the past twenty years into one contiguous block. No one planned it; it just unfolded that way. To say I was humbled by what life had done this time would be an understatement.

I built a wooden boardwalk that connected my new house to the Temple's existing boardwalk, and this became my new commute to work. Some time later Mataji came to visit, and I showed her the house. In her quiet voice she said, "So God called you one day and said, 'Mickey, your house is ready.'" I think that pretty much sums it up.

Life calls me on the phone one day and says,
"Mickey, your house is ready."

My commute to work—truly amazing.

40.

The Scary Messenger
of Change

I settled into my new house in the spring of 1991, and it seemed like I was living a dream. I was completely content with everything around me: family, business, and the Temple community. The perfection of what I was surrounded by was enough to challenge the rational mind. And I was always aware that I had never asked for any of it—I was living in a life made by the flow of life.

I can look back now and see the exact moment when the winds ushering in the next period of change first blew across my face. I didn't understand what was coming at the time, but at least I knew enough to embrace whatever was taking place. I had already learned time and again that it didn't matter if I understood what was happening; it was sufficient to devote myself to the present moment and trust that the flow of life knew what it was doing. The flow of events that happened next was so miraculous that it had the effect of permanently freeing me from an entire layer of my personal mind. If life could pull off these events, how could I not completely surrender to her perfection?

Before we begin, however, I have a confession to make: I cannot foretell the future. There was no possible way I could have known that in order to keep up with Personalized Programming's destined growth, it would not be sufficient to double or even triple my current twenty-five employees; I would need to grow to more than three hundred employees. What is more, I could never have imagined that our building needs would have to grow from our current forty-three hundred square feet to over eighty-five thousand square feet to provide for what was coming. If someone had tried to tell me this back in the early '90s, I would have considered them crazy! Yet to grow like that, there had better be some planning. Apparently there was, but it certainly wasn't by me.

This amazing story of how life's perfection provided for our future growth began one Friday afternoon when a zoning inspector suddenly showed up at our office. He seemed very surprised to see a business out here in the woods, and he told me to call his boss, the head of county zoning, right away. That was how it all started, and it seemed very ominous.

I knew the head of zoning from my work with Built with Love. I gave him a call, and after some pleasantries he explained to me that even though the public was not frequenting my business location, I did not have the required zoning for a business out here. I explored possible solutions with him, including getting the zoning changed or obtaining a special exception permit, all to no avail. To make his point ironclad, he told me that due to the state land usage plan, even if my father were president of the United States and I had a million dollars to spend on the effort—I could not get legal business zoning on any part of our property.

Realizing that I would be in big trouble if he shut me down, I shifted to damage control. I told him that I appreciated his position and asked him what I should do. He told me to start looking for a piece of land down on the main highway since that would be the closest business zoning to our property. My heart dropped as I realized that this little piece of heaven that had come together organically over the years was about to change. The main highway was a minimum of three miles away, and the distance to available property would likely be much greater.

I took a deep breath, raised my chin up, and gave him my word that I would take care of the problem. I requested a reasonable amount of time to find the land and make the move. He didn't promise me anything but said he would be checking back with me to be sure we were coming into compliance with the requirements.

This is how life managed to not so subtly nudge me into looking for a new business location. The moment I hung up, I went into Rick Karl's office to get his legal advice. Rick agreed that we had no real basis out here in the middle of agricultural zoning to get spot zoning for a small business. So we called a Realtor to start looking for the closest possible business property. I, of course, didn't want to move the business from the Temple, but my experiment with surrender meant I had to stay open and see where the flow of life's events would lead me. Months went by, one after another, but nothing suitable showed up. With each passage of time, the risk increased that the county would shut us down. Nonetheless, I was patiently waiting for life to make her move.

In September of that year, life made her next move. We received a phone call from the person who had sold us the beautiful eighty-five-acre piece of property a year earlier. He now wanted to sell the adjoining fifty acres that ran up to the paved county road. It fit in perfectly with the Temple property, so we went ahead and bought it. There was no way at the time we could have ever imagined that this purchase would end up related to Personalized Programming's search for legal business zoning. We were just dealing with what was put in front of us.

A few months later another property event unfolded that we had to deal with. It seemed that someone was planning to build a 185-acre construction waste dump directly across the street from the fifty acres the Temple had just purchased. We looked into the matter and were shocked to find that it was true. The piece of land had been annexed into the City of Alachua years ago and was no longer under county zoning. The land was owned by a prominent city commissioner, and he had recently sold it to be used as a construction waste dump. It was projected that for the next twenty years, a hundred large dump trucks would be driving down our road seven days a week and dumping on property directly adjoining ours and our neighbors'. So much for the flow of life—I thought we were supposed to be led into green pastures, not garbage dumps!

The neighborhood was in an uproar. The Temple was the largest landowner in the area, and people started asking us what to do. We looked into it, and it appeared that the City of Alachua had the authority to grant a special use permit for a waste dump—if city commissioners chose to do so. We really had no choice but to focus our attention on this matter, to the detriment of the search for our new office property.

We decided that our best course of action was to write a letter informing the citizens of Alachua that since there was no comprehensive waste management plan for the city, a dump could be placed anywhere, including on the vacant lot next to their house. The goal was to push the city into passing a comprehensive waste management plan instead of arbitrarily issuing special use permits, as they were about to do for this dump.

Believe it or not, it actually worked. The night of the city commissioners' meeting on the topic, City Hall was jam-packed with a standing-room-only crowd. Before calling the meeting to order, the mayor stood up and told everyone not to worry because there was not going to be a vote on a special use permit tonight, or any other night, until the city passed a comprehensive waste management plan. The commission thanked the citizens for their input and committed to working on a plan as soon as possible.

Little did we know that our victory regarding the garbage dump was really life's miraculous hand taking care of Personalized Programming's zoning issue. A few days later, we got a call informing us that because the waste dump did not get its permit, the 185-acre piece of property had suddenly come up for sale at a very reasonable price. Since the property was in the City of Alachua, we were told that it was possible to get it zoned for business usage. I will never forget Rick's face when he walked into my office to tell me of his conversation with the Realtor. The impossible had happened—the flow of life had just unfolded in a way that led to a phone call telling us that instead of a waste dump adjoining Temple property, we could put our business there. Rick and I just sat in silence for a while. The feeling of awe and grace in that room was so powerful that neither of us could move, let alone speak.

Just look at what Rick and I had witnessed in the past six months. First, life had informed me, in no uncertain terms, that I had to leave my office on Temple property and find a new location. When I tried to comply, nothing would fall into place. Then, out of the blue, we were presented with a piece of land that would ultimately connect Temple property to our future office property, without us having the slightest idea of what was really going on. The flow of life then presented us with what appeared to be a terrible situation wherein someone was preparing to build a waste dump adjoining our property. But what was really going on was that life was preparing to give us a great gift— the most perfect piece of land for Personalized Programming's future. This land adjoined Temple property and could get legal business zoning, something we had previously been told was impossible out here where we lived. And let's not forget that all this happened while I only had twenty-five employees and could not possibly have known that I would ever need anything like this—but apparently life knew, and she certainly took good care of us. So it came to be. Personalized Programming now had legal business zoning on property adjoining the Temple's land. It was time to build.

With so much land having come in such a miraculous manner, I was forced to rethink my plans for the size of the new office building. I stretched my thoughts into the realm of building something that assured that we would never have to build again. We designed a beautiful, 14,500-square-foot office building that was worthy of a company as successful as Personalized Programming. Built with Love, which I had sold many years ago to one of my job foremen, built the building, and it turned out exquisite. In June 1993, Personalized Programming moved its twenty-five employees just down the road to their new home. We moved from 4,300 square feet to 14,500—at least we would never have to build again.

Amazingly, that did not turn out to be the case. Over the next year we more than doubled in size and had to start planning for another building. Building 2 was even larger than Building 1 and adjoined to it with a covered walkway. It's a good thing that life had given us enough land to handle this totally unexpected expansion. By the time it was all done, we ended up with five buildings, giving us more than 85,000 square feet of high-tech office space. To this day, I stand in awe of how life unfolded so perfectly to provide us exactly what we needed, exactly when we needed it.

*Personalized Programming, 1993. They said it was
impossible, yet life manifests this gorgeous new
office building bordering Temple property. What an
amazing flow of events!*

*Medical Manager Corporation R&D facility, 2003.
Life even knew enough to allow for undreamed
of expansion—from one building to a pristine
five-building office campus.*

41.

The Foundation Is Built
for the Future

Personalized Programming's growth was astonishing. With it came all the problems associated with a rapidly growing technology company. Managing ten to twenty people is one thing, managing fifty-five is quite another. At some point you have to start hiring managers just to manage the people. I resisted creating middle management as much as possible. I tried to let the teams manage themselves with my constant guidance. Because we had grown from the ground up, and very few of my people ever left, we had a tremendous wealth of technical and industry knowledge in our programming group. With twenty-five percent of all independent physicians across the United States using The Medical Manager, the practice management industry flowed through Alachua, Florida. We didn't have to decide what direction to go in; we were surfers riding the powerful wave of industry demand. There was so much work to do that it was almost impossible to keep up.

By late 1994, I began to realize that I couldn't possibly run all the programming groups and the financial and management aspects of a multimillion-dollar business, as well as prepare for the next wave of growth. I needed some serious help. So I did what I always did—worked even harder and waited for the flow of life to do its thing.

It was in this backdrop that I first met Tim Staley. Tim was a professional software developer and senior IT consultant who had decided to move his family out to the country. He had chosen the tiny town of

High Springs, just a few miles north of Alachua, as his new home. If you're a professional IT person and you move out to my neck of the woods, you are certainly going to hear about Personalized Programming. Tim applied for a job just like anyone else would. But Tim was not like anyone else—Tim was another miracle. Just like everything else that showed up exactly when it was supposed to, life had dropped this highly skilled and experienced IT developer/executive in my lap. He would not only end up being the solution to the software development problems we were having, he would also end up being the solution to a much larger problem that hadn't even surfaced yet.

I remember the first time I met Tim. He was in a rush to find employment in the area so he could move his family up before school started for his children. After seeing his résumé, I allowed HR to set up a Saturday meeting so Tim did not have to miss work. He was young, very clean and proper looking, and in his right hand he was carrying a bible. That's an unusual thing to bring to a job interview, but Tim was clearly a very religious Christian, and he wanted me to know it. I had no problem with that, but I was not sure that he would not have a problem with a ponytailed, sandal-wearing yogi for a boss.

We went up to my office, and we began to get to know each other. Tim was, in fact, a rocket scientist. He had worked for years at Harris Corporation writing code for missile guidance systems. I immediately realized I could check off the "smart enough" box. He had been a developer, team leader, and project manager. Tim excelled so thoroughly at his overall project development and people skills that he was now a senior consultant for Texas Instruments running large projects for clients. Interestingly, at that time he was consulting on a major IT project for Blue Cross Blue Shield of Florida.

We began to discuss development philosophy, and we were as different as the way we dressed. To me, software development was a creative art—to him it was an engineering project. The truth is, I knew it had to be both in order to be successful in the long run. Tim clearly brought to the table the experiential discipline that comes from being a senior software engineer in a Fortune 500 technology company. We were desperately in need of that knowledge and experience.

Tim and I spent hours together and really got to like each other. He was a perfect fit for what Personalized Programming needed, both professionally and personally. But I still had one issue that needed to be resolved. If Tim was going to seriously consider taking the job, I needed to be sure he was going to be comfortable with who I was. At some point he was certainly going to hear about the Temple across the street. I decided the only fair thing to do was to take him over there and show him around.

I was amazed by how open Tim was to the Temple. He was fascinated by the artifacts of the various religions and asked a lot of deep questions about meditation and yoga. It turned out that Tim was much more than a very religious person—he was deeply spiritual and was truly a lover of God. Rather than being offended by how I had come up, he was inspired by it. A very deep spiritual bond formed that day as we shared our spiritual experiences and beliefs with each other. This bond of spiritual friendship grew stronger and stronger over the next ten years that we worked together. Apparently, life had outdone itself once again

I hired Tim, and we decided to quietly bring him in as a developer instead of as top management. He wanted to work directly with my people to get to know the development environment firsthand. The plan was that after some months he would start to reorganize and take charge of the development teams. I would remain in charge of product direction; he would be in charge of engineering. I couldn't wait to find out how much of the load Tim would be capable of carrying.

The Medical Manager product was more than fifteen years old by the time Tim began working with it. It had been designed for small doctor practices and was now being used to run large clinics and sprawling managed care organizations. It was not unusual for some of our larger dealers to install systems that supported hundreds of users. If this kept up, we would eventually outgrow the technical capabilities of the software. In addition, our clients were beginning to ask us to modernize the overall product. The writing was on the wall: unless we did something, our days were numbered. If we wanted a solid foundation for the future, we were going to have to completely rewrite the product.

This was not a decision for the faint of heart. It was going to take a tremendous investment, putting at risk years of development resources and millions of dollars. As I pondered over the enormity of the project that lay before us, it finally hit me—this was the real reason that Tim had been sent to us. He had been sent to reengineer The Medical Manager into a totally new product with the latest development technology.

We couldn't afford to stop the rapid pace of development of the existing system, so I gave Tim the go-ahead to hire an entire additional development team to build the new product. Intergy would be the new product's name, and it was a good thing we were building more buildings because we were certainly going to need them. I trusted Tim implicitly and gave him whatever he asked for. It took us close to five years to release the new product, but when all was said and done, we ended up with a product that would keep us in the marketplace for many years to come. As I look back now, it is so obvious that we could never have succeeded as we did without Tim showing up exactly when he did. How in the world does this keep happening, again and again?

42.

Meanwhile—
Back at the Ranch

There was so much work to do at Personalized Programming that I pretty much worked all my waking hours—except for my mornings and evenings in the Temple. The Temple community was so stable that it hardly took any of my management time. Radha was able to manage the Temple and its finances even though her position as the chief financial controller at Personalized Programming kept her working day and night. In the midst of all this transformation, the Temple was about to experience a change of its own.

At the end of 1994, Amrit had a major falling-out with his followers. As is the case with so many people we put up on a pedestal, some inappropriate behavior from his past came to light, and the situation proved extremely difficult for everyone. When I heard that Amrit had actually left the community, I invited him and his wife to come spend some quiet time living with us at the Temple. To be there when a person is soaring high is an easy relationship. To be there during hard times requires deep friendship. All of us had received a great deal from Amrit over the years. We were humbled at the opportunity to give something back.

Radha had been living in the Jenkins house for several years by then. Since it was the nicest house on our property, she immediately offered to move out. In December 1994, Amrit and his wife moved into that house and ended up living there for the better part of three years. It was an amazing experience to be that close to such an evolved person going through such a life-changing experience. While he was here, Amrit simply allowed the situation to put him through whatever changes he needed to go through. Situations like this are like fire, and Amrit just wanted to use that fire for spiritual purification. He wasn't sad, he wasn't hurt, and he wasn't scared—he was just completely surrendered to going through the experience. I constantly saw in Amrit what I always saw inside of me: when push comes to shove, I don't care what it takes, just free me from myself. The only meaningful prayer is that this white-hot fire be so destructive to the personal self that it severs the cord that binds. Standing soul to soul, Amrit and I had that in common—liberation at any cost.

I didn't isolate myself from what Amrit was going through. I wanted to share the experience of exploring what it would be like inside if everything were taken away outside. I recalled King Solomon's wisdom: *For every thing there is a season, a time for every purpose under heaven.* I had been honored to know Amrit as a world-renowned teacher; I was now all the more honored to be close to him as he passed through a period of great darkness or, better put, as a period of great darkness passed through him. He never complained, and he never got depressed or despondent. He just spent each day surrendering at a deeper and deeper level. Reality was what it was—might as well use it to let go of the personal self.

As with all things, in time the energy began to shift. The noise of the past subsided and opportunities for the future began to open up. One day Amrit asked me to take a drive with him to see a place he had found in the Ocala National Forest. It was in a very small town less than an hour and a half south of the Temple. I couldn't believe the place when I saw it. It was an absolutely beautiful giant house sitting on the shore of a gorgeous lake, and there were also five or six cabins on the property. It was a perfect home for Amrit and his family. Every place I walked, I felt Amrit. I had known him for years, and I knew his taste. You could not have custom built a home specifically for him that was more perfect than this place. I had to hold back tears as I realized—it was over. The period of darkness had passed. I encouraged him to buy the property if he could afford it. He then told me the price. I couldn't believe my ears—it was the deal of the century.

I learned a lot about surrender by being with Amrit during this whole ordeal. What I saw was that no matter who we are, life is going to put us through the changes we need to go through. The question is: Are we willing to use this force for our transformation? I saw that even very intense situations don't have to leave psychological scars, if we are willing to process our changes at a deeper level. My surrender experiment had already taught me to deeply honor the transformative power of life. Sharing that time with Amrit would prove to be all the more important since life as I knew it was once again about to go through a major, unexpected change.

Section VIII

Embracing Explosive

Expansion

43.

The Medical Manager
Sprouts Wings

I f you had asked me in 1995 what I thought the future of Personalized Programming looked like, I would have told you that we had
grown about as big as we could, and the challenge was going to
be staying at the top of our industry. If you had asked me about my
surrender experiment, I would have told you that the relentless practice
of letting go of myself in order to fully embrace what was unfolding
around me was having a profound effect on my spiritual growth. It
had, in fact, become my way of life. I had seen time and again that letting go not only led to amazing results, but it also left me in a state of
profound inner peace. I was not in charge; life was in charge, and there
was an underlying sense of enthusiasm and excitement about getting
to see what was going to happen next. After all, just look at what had
happened so far.

By the end of 1995, Personalized Programming had grown to
seventy-five employees and had enough work to keep us busy for a
very long time. I loved what we were doing, and we were obviously
very good at it. Our revenues had reached ten million dollars a year,
and since most of that was royalty payments, we were profiting five to
six million a year. The Medical Manager itself was more than fifteen
years old by then, and it was touching the lives of hundreds of thousands of people. In my limited view of things, I saw us going on like
this for the foreseeable future.

The first clue that dramatic change was once again on the horizon came when I learned that Systems Plus and many of the dealers were discussing the possibility of merging together into one company. Apparently, they felt this would help them compete better at the national level. Soon afterward, I received a visit from one of our larger dealers, John Kang, who was headquartered in Tampa. He informed me that he had been working on a proposal to consolidate the Medical Manager dealers into a combined company. He laid out his plan of initially purchasing Personalized Programming, Systems Plus, and three or four of the larger dealerships. He explained that it would take a large initial investment, but he already had that lined up. John's presentation was very professional, but I didn't see why Personalized Programming had to be involved. I told him that I would be willing to legally commit to providing The Medical Manager software to the new company. He then dropped the bombshell: any investors in the company would insist that the foundational software be owned by the company itself.

I was very uncomfortable with the thought of selling Personalized Programming. But I was even more uncomfortable thinking that I would be the reason that all these hundreds of dealers, and Systems Plus, were unable to get their hard-earned value from their businesses. I told John I was not interested in selling the business at any price, but if my reluctance was truly in the way of everyone else's dreams, I would have to give his proposal some consideration. I told him he could come back to see me if he succeeded in getting others to buy in to his plan. What I was really hoping, however, was that the whole thing would just fall through by itself.

John returned a few weeks later having obtained buy-in from some of our largest dealers as well as Systems Plus. The handwriting was on the wall—this was becoming like all the previous times I had to put aside my strong personal preferences and surrender to what was manifesting before me. I didn't like it one bit, but I was fully committed to seeing where the path of surrender to life was going to lead me.

John Kang made me a persuasive offer for Personalized Programming that included both cash and stock in the new company. He then set out on the difficult journey of merging five businesses into one and raising the funds needed to pull the merger off. The bankers decided it would be best to raise the necessary $150 million by selling shares of the new company publicly. The date for an initial public offering (IPO) was set for early 1997, but a lot of work still needed to be done.

What a world to be thrown into. Personalized Programming had grown gradually from its humble roots of one employee—me. It was now a very well organized, highly successful private company. This level of organization was not going to exist when a bunch of independently run businesses first get thrown into a pot together. There were going to be the expected power struggles, dealer acquisition issues, and constant legal and financial issues to be ironed out. Nonetheless, I didn't allow myself to get caught up in all those negative thoughts. I just remained open and completely intrigued by what was unfolding.

It was decided that the new company would be called Medical Manager Corporation. I must admit, I liked that. I flashed back to 1981 when I was finishing the software and first came up with the name "The Medical Manager." Fifteen years later, Medical Manager was now going to become a public company. Standing at the threshold of this major event, I was totally in awe seeing where my experiment with surrender had managed to lead me.

44

Medical Manager
Corporation—MMGR

When the smoke cleared, I was to be the chief executive officer (CEO); John Kang, the president; and Rick Karl, the general counsel. Corporate headquarters would be established in Tampa at John Kang's facilities, and Rick Karl and I would work out of the Alachua offices. The company would trade on the NASDAQ exchange under the symbol MMGR.

As we headed toward the end of 1996, the cadre of lawyers and bankers was finishing up all the paperwork to merge the companies together and simultaneously do the IPO. I remember that this was an interesting time for me in my relationship with my dad. My father had been a stockbroker most of his life, and he had been working at Merrill Lynch for more than thirty years. His only son had dropped out of graduate school in business to live in the woods and meditate. I never left the woods, yet all of a sudden I was in my dad's world. He kept telling me that he just couldn't believe that Morgan Stanley, one of the premiere brokerage houses in the world, was interested in my company. He was also surprised to find out that Merrill Lynch's health-care analyst was closely monitoring our upcoming transaction. My dad was very interested that my company was going public, and we talked to each other more during this time than we had for the previous twenty years put together. It makes sense—we now had something in common to talk about.

I was humbled by this opportunity to get closer to my father. I saw it as just another miraculous thing that had happened as I surrendered to the flow of life. It wasn't too much later when my dad died. But you can be sure he enjoyed being able to give his son his lifetime-learned advice about becoming a public company, the health-care sector, and Wall Street in general.

Despite the amazing sequence of events that led up to this point, nothing could have prepared me for what happened next. A week or so before the IPO, I received a list of action items from my New York attorney. One by one I worked through the list, signing required documents and locating required paperwork. The final item was due the next day, so I rushed down to my bank to access my safety deposit box. I rarely had reason to touch this box I had rented back in 1971 to store my only possession—the deed for my original ten acres.

Once I was left alone with the storage box, I began looking for the document my attorney had requested. There wasn't much in the box, but what was there had the effect of a time machine. I came across the original deed on my property—how much had happened since then. No one in their right mind could have imagined the flow of events that unfolded since I decided to drop out and live in the woods. My trip back in time was interrupted when I came upon the document I was looking for. I pulled out the trifolded piece of paper and opened it up. It was the Personalized Programming stock certificate sent to me when I incorporated the company fifteen years earlier. When I had originally dropped the certificate in my deposit box, it was pretty much worthless to anyone but me. Then it hit me like a ton of bricks. The most savvy investors in the world were valuing this piece of paper at over a hundred million dollars.

My mouth went dry, and tears welled up in my eyes. I had given everything up, and it kept coming back tenfold. When I had decided to let go and devote my life to serving what was unfolding in front of me, I was earning less than five thousand dollars a year. When Built with Love came together, it grew from tens of thousands to hundreds of thousands in revenue. When Personalized Programming came together, it quickly grew to millions and then more than ten million in sales and royalties. Now I was dealing with a hundred-million-dollar asset. It wasn't the money that moved me; it was the invisible hand of life that blew me away. I stood there in the bank and offered that piece of paper back to the universe from whence it had come. I vowed to serve the company I had watched life build, brick by brick, and to use the money entrusted to me in a way that would help others. I took a deep breath, closed the deposit box, and prepared to ship the stock certificate up to New York.

45

Becoming CEO

Medical Manager Corporation was born out of a successful IPO on February 2, 1997. Out here in the woods of Alachua, not only did I maintain my position as president of our large R&D facility, but I also became CEO and chairman of the board of directors of the new company. I was completely naive as to how much work I would be taking on as CEO. I quickly realized that it was going to require all the one-pointed focus I had developed through my years of meditation. I had surrendered, and this was the task life had given me. That made it part of my spiritual journey, and I was fully prepared to devote myself to it to the absolute best of my ability.

The first thing I did was take the steps necessary to assure that I would know what was going on in the company. I was in Alachua, and a group of independent-minded executives accustomed to running their own businesses were scattered around the country. If I was going to take responsibility for the company, a thorough flow of information needed to pass across my desk. This was going to require regular group conference calls and an enormous amount of reporting to keep up with what everyone was doing. When I announced that each executive had to turn in a weekly report on the major activities under their domain, there was definitely some grumbling. But together we had an enormous amount of experience, and I wanted the group-mind making decisions, not any one person's mind.

It wasn't long, however, before I realized that I couldn't possibly keep up with all the weekly status reports plus be properly prepared for the executive conference calls. I needed some serious help, and as you may have guessed by now, that is exactly what I got.

We won't call it a miracle, but this time life's magic showed up in the form of a young lady named Sabrina. Paul Dobbins had met her years earlier at one of our national dealer seminars, and apparently, it was love at first sight. Not too long after that, Paul informed us that Sabrina was moving here, and they were getting married. I didn't know Sabrina, and I was concerned that Paul expected her to move into a yoga-based spiritual community when she wasn't even into yoga or meditation. He assured me that she would fit in just fine, and he also informed me that I would be very pleased to have her work at the company. Surrender, surrender, surrender—like I had a choice.

As it turns out, Sabrina's family business was a small Medical Manager dealership in California. She had been selling, installing, and supporting practice management software since she was thirteen years old. Though she was only twenty-two when she began working at Personalized Programming, and had never even been to college, I soon found out that senior-level business analysis was completely natural to her. Despite the fact that she had no prior experience at this level, Sabrina was the person I turned to for executive help when I became CEO.

With Sabrina at my side, one of my main responsibilities as CEO became growing the company. Fortunately, this was no ordinary company; the prospects for growth in the newly created Medical Manager Corporation were phenomenal. To start with, our growth would come naturally as we acquired our dealers. We had close to two hundred dealers, many of which would be very good acquisitions for us. As long as we had a steady stream of new dealers merging into the company, we had a natural source of growth.

Much more interesting to me, however, was the tremendous growth that could come from our ability to electronically connect our enormous number of doctors to the rest of the health-care industry, including insurance companies, laboratories, and pharmacies. Once we rolled support of our practices under one roof, we could provide a level of automation for the health-care system that would not only cut costs but also result in improved efficiency and patient care.

I sat down with Sabrina and told her that getting our hundred-thousand-plus doctors fully up on electronic claims and other health-care transactions was going to be our first new corporate business initiative. I then informed her that she was going to be in charge. This was the birth of what we called Medical Manager Network Services. The success of this venture at so many levels was practically incomprehensible. It started out as an inspired vision and grew into a $100-million-a-year line of business. In a very short period of time, we led the industry in electronic transactions.

Over the next two years, the company grew by leaps and bounds. We kept acquiring more and more of our dealers, and our nationwide presence meant we could provide our services to larger and larger clients. Meanwhile, I never worked so hard in my life. But it didn't burn me out. In fact, it had the opposite effect. The more I let go of "Mickey" and just committed myself to the task life had given me, the more the spiritual energy flow increased within me. It was as though by aligning myself with life's outer flow, the beautiful, inward flow of energy was naturally strengthened. By now, I had become thoroughly convinced that the constant act of letting go of one's self-centered thoughts and emotions was all that was needed for profound personal, professional, and spiritual growth.

46

The Internet and
Health Care

After almost thirty years, I'd seen enough perfection unfold around me that nothing in me wanted to interfere with the flow ever again. I had seen time and again how what at first appeared to be a problem turned out to be a guiding force of change leading us forward. That was certainly the case toward the end of 1998 as our executive strategy calls began to focus on how the Internet was going to affect our business. It concerned us that our competitors would soon have inexpensive access to all physicians nationwide without the need to build out a dealer network. John Kang and I were well aware that two health-care Internet companies, Healtheon and WebMD, were already soliciting our doctors on an ever-increasing basis. We knew we had to do something if we wanted to be able to compete successfully in the upcoming world of Internet connectivity.

Around this time, John Kang had been introduced to a company called Synetic, in New Jersey, that was in the process of building a very advanced health-care Internet portal. Synetic had one of the finest management teams in the industry, and it appeared that none of the other start-up companies stood a chance against it.

Synetic executives were very interested in a possible merger with Medical Manager Corporation. Their dream was to handle all the industry's health-care transactions through their Internet portal. When they looked at us, they saw more than one hundred thousand physicians already connected electronically for a broad range of services. If they handled the transactions for all our physicians, everyone in the industry would want to do business with them. Synetic was in a position to leverage the asset we had built to an entirely new level.

In May of 1999, John Kang set up a meeting for me to meet Synetic's chairman, Marty Wygod. Marty and I lived on opposite sides of the country, so he suggested that we meet at an aptly named private airport in Midway, Texas. Midway was, in fact, almost exactly halfway between California and Florida. I chartered a private jet and flew in by myself.

Sitting alone in a six-seater jet at forty thousand feet is a very peaceful place. I fell into meditation and my mind became very still. When I opened my eyes, I absorbed the tremendous difference in my environment from when I had first decided to let go and see where life would take me. I still lived in the same woods and kept my same practices morning and evening, but somehow the rest had changed rather dramatically. I reflected back at how many times life had presented me with changes I was uncomfortable with. In the beginning, it had been difficult to ignore the resistant mind. Over time, as I saw what had transpired by taking the risk of letting go of me, the process had become much more natural. I was surrounded by the results of letting go. There was nothing in my life I could point to that hadn't come from surrendering to life's flow. I was so humbled by the process that nothing in me wanted to resist ever again. I was deeply in love with the excitement and wonder of experiencing what would unfold next. It was in this frame of mind that I was off to Texas to meet Synetic's chairman.

To me, this proposed merger was simply what was happening next. I didn't need to think about it; I already knew that nothing inside of me wanted to merge the company with Synetic or anyone else. I loved what I was doing. I had a vision burning inside of me that had driven me for twenty years. It started while I was first writing this amazing program, and it never subsided for a single moment. That vision inspired me day and night. I didn't want to eat, and I didn't want to sleep. I was driven to perfect the program, its distribution, and the support of the doctors who had entrusted their practices to us. I felt like life had given me this task, and I was honored to do it. I had not lost one drop of my early focus or yearning to explore the deeper inner states. This surrendering to life *was* my path to self-realization, and there was no doubt that it was working. I was not living a life based on what I wanted or didn't want. Those types of thoughts had ceased passing through my mind long ago. I was way too busy trying to do the work life had given me. This was Karma yoga at its highest. I had given my life to the Universal Flow, and it had not only taken it— it had devoured me in the process. I didn't care at all what happened to me. I cared about the company, the employees, the doctors, and, above all, the vision of perfection that drove the very beat of my heart.

As beautiful as that sounds, I found myself on a jet flying to a tiny airport somewhere in the middle of Texas to meet a total stranger and discuss arrangements to put the company under his control. That was the bottom line. Events had unfolded such that the greatest potential for the company had outgrown what we could provide by ourselves. My discussions with John Kang about the proposed deal had shown me how sharp Marty was. Control was definitely my major issue. I wanted to be in a position to keep the dream alive and protect the company from being abused for strictly financial gain. Marty had agreed to put John, me, and some other Medical Manager Corporation board members on the board of directors of the combined company. He also agreed to make me co-chairman of the board, and John and I would become the co-CEOs. For added incentive, the new combined company would keep our name, Medical Manager Corporation.

Though I was a novice at mergers of public companies, I was astute enough to know what granting us these high-level positions really meant. It meant that Marty was so confident of his position of power that he did not feel the slightest bit threatened by ceding this amount of power to people with whom he had no history. Any way you cut it, if the deal went through, Marty was going to be my boss. This was all the more interesting since I never really had a boss before, and I was fifty-two years old. I had researched all I could about Marty. He was a self-made billionaire who bred and raced thoroughbred horses for a hobby. He had grown up on Wall Street buying and selling companies, and he had also built some very successful companies from the ground up, including Medco, which he had sold to Merck pharmaceuticals for six billion dollars years earlier. Most important, he was highly respected in the upper echelons of business. More than one article about him freely used the term "genius."

Marty had made an offer of $1.3 billion for Medical Manager Corporation. Our board of directors was leaning very favorably toward the deal. I felt pretty certain that all vectors were flowing in that direction—that's why I was flying out for this meeting. What I didn't know was what life would be like in this larger corporate environment. I realized I could never know beforehand, and I was ready to surrender once again to the flow of life. From a personal point of view, I was much more interested in seeing how Marty did with me than how I did with him. I was a ponytailed, non-suit-wearing yogi, and Marty was sure to be a more traditional businessman. Was this going to work?

Marty flew in on his jet with one of his business development people. The meeting lasted only a few hours and everything went fine, as would be expected under these circumstances. We each had already spent sufficient time analyzing the proposed merger, so by the time we met, the synergies were quite clear. I found Marty to be very down to earth and approachable. He was all business, and I really liked that. I made a point of discussing (or more accurately—disclosing) the existence of the Temple, and my commitment to meditation and my alternative lifestyle. I knew I wasn't going to give any of that up, so it seemed appropriate to let him know what he was getting into. It was obvious that Marty was way past the small stuff. He was a big picture person, and what he cared about was corporate development. He couldn't have cared less about my personal lifestyle, but he paid close attention when I discussed how hard I worked every day. He told me his wife did yoga, and I figured that being from California he was bound to have been exposed to the likes of me. As Marty and I shook hands and went our own ways, there was no way I could have known how much I would end up learning, both personally and professionally, from this man.

47

Merging—But Not
with the Universe

Over the years, I had come to see that I really had no idea where life was going to put me on any given day. And, in truth, it was none of my business. My job was to simply continue surrendering and serving what was put in front of me. Such was the case on the day I found myself chairing a Medical Manager Corporation board meeting specifically called to discuss the proposed merger with Synetic.

Medical Manager had a very active board of directors, many of whom had tremendous business experience, including a previous treasurer of General Motors. The board was seriously considering our various options going forward. We had done $140 million of business the previous year versus Synetic's $70 million. But the tremendous potential value of its web portal had pushed Synetic's market value way beyond ours and made the company an attractive partner. In the end, the board unanimously decided to accept Synetic's $1.3 billion offer for the company.

I, of course, had never been involved in a billion-dollar merger before. But we had great outside counsel and a good team of bankers to assist us. I turned to Sabrina to work by my side on this enormous project. Marty had put the merger on the fast track, and all the details had to be worked out in a few weeks. We worked day and night to get the final deal presented to both boards, and the merger was announced publicly on May 17, 1999.

The merger between Medical Manager Corporation and Synetic created quite a stir. It was the main business story on CNN that evening and was prominent in the *Wall Street Journal* the next day. The new company kept the Medical Manager Corporation name, and John Kang and I were co-CEOs and sat on the board of directors with Marty as chairman. Though I still lived at the Temple of the Universe and simply drove across the street to get to work, my world had instantly expanded. My responsibilities now stretched beyond the practice management business and included all the areas of business Marty's team had been working on. In truth, that was the most exciting part of the merger. I now had an entire team of world-class executives to work with. Marty surrounded himself with the best of the best, and it was really an honor to get to work with these people.

As it turned out, Synetic's main competitors were our old friends, WebMD and Healtheon, who had merged together by now. Their combined company provided serious competition for our health-care Internet portal. The question was simply one of time—would there be enough time for us to build out our highly sophisticated web offering before Healtheon/WebMD attracted too much of the available funding?

The answer to that question came on January 25, 2000, just six months after our merger with Synetic. We awoke to the news that Healtheon/WebMD had managed to acquire Envoy, the largest claims clearinghouse in the industry, for $2.5 billion. That was quite an acquisition considering that Healtheon/WebMD was a web start-up company reporting enormous losses, and Envoy was a well-established, highly profitable clearinghouse for health-care transactions. It was quickly determined that we could not maintain a competitive position in light of this deal. From Medical Manager's point of view, the deal meant that our competitor now owned the clearinghouse through which we were channeling all of our clients' hundreds of millions of claims a year. There were times when I was very glad I was no longer in charge—late January 2000 was definitely one of them.

48

Building Rome in a Day

M arty was calm and collected at the ensuing board meeting. In fact, he seemed even sharper than usual. It turned out he was just as good at playing downside situations as he was at leveraging upside opportunities. He went over the options with the board, and it was decided we had best try to negotiate a decent merger agreement with Healtheon/WebMD. It was a classic case of "if you can't beat them, join them." The problem was that we were well aware that the underpinnings of Healtheon/WebMD were very weak. The company had been built up based solely on the vision of future performance, yet the market was valuing it at $7 billion. Unfortunately, our most promising road to success meant merging with them and doing the hard work necessary to make it all a reality.

As unbelievable as it seems, Medical Manager Corporation and Healtheon/WebMD announced their merger agreement just three weeks after we learned of the Envoy deal. It was on Valentine's Day, February 14, 2000. The deal valued Medical Manager Corporation at $3.5 billion, and Wall Street characterized it as the merger of two behemoths in the health-care industry. It drew headlines everywhere. The announcement pushed Medical Manager's stock price to a peak of $86 a share. This can be compared to $17.60 per share when we went public three years earlier.

The joy was short-lived. The infamous Internet bubble, caused by overinflated expectations for Internet companies, began to burst just weeks after the merger announcement. We had not even closed the deal, yet by April 2000, Healtheon/WebMD had already lost 70 percent of its value. Our stock fell accordingly because it was tied to their stock by the merger agreement. It was all pretty much a disaster, and the only hope left was to do the hard work necessary to restructure the entire company.

The task was Herculean. WebMD was the quintessential Internet company, and the Internet bubble had just burst. WebMD's stock had once traded above $100 per share. It was at $17.50 when we closed the deal, on its way to a low of $3 in August 2001. This called for drastic measures, and that is what it got.

Within a month of closing, Marty became chairman of the board, and he and his elite management team were running the company. I remained CEO of the Practice Services Division and sat on the board of directors of the combined company, which kept the name WebMD. Marty brought in a seasoned turnaround specialist, Marv Rich, to be president during the massive reorganization. The company was losing hundreds of millions of dollars a year and the bleeding had to be stopped. Marv's job was to work his way through all the divisions and cut them down to core competency. All that would remain was that which aligned with WebMD's core vision and could quickly begin earning its keep.

The task before us was breathtaking, and it provided tremendous growth for me, personally. I now found myself part of a team of executives who, instead of complaining, simply rolled up their sleeves and tackled this monumental project. Everyone was working day and night to do whatever was needed to right the sinking ship. For years I had been diligently working to free myself of that weak person inside who always insisted on things being the way he wanted. Now, nothing was the way anybody would have wanted. Yet everyone just took a collective deep breath and did whatever was asked of them. It was an amazing thing to be part of, and it taught me a lesson of inner strength that permanently changed me at a very deep level.

Marv called me one day and asked me to accompany him to California where the WebMD Internet site was being developed. If the company we had merged with had a main asset, this was it. Marv wanted me to act as a development specialist at meetings with the website's development team. Most of the company's losses were being generated by its Internet offerings, and this had to be dealt with. The problem was that, despite the losses, the development team was making enormous demands for salaries and benefits from the new WebMD management. They figured they were in the driver's seat since they controlled the development of the company's entire Internet offering.

I couldn't believe what I saw when we arrived. More than eight hundred developers were working in a giant converted warehouse in Silicon Valley. It was tiny cubicle after tiny cubicle as far as the eye could see. I thought my development team in Alachua had expanded tremendously. We were around 250 people, but this development team was over three times that size, and everyone was packed in like sardines.

Unfortunately, the meetings didn't last very long. Marv and I sat with their senior management team and listened to their demands. They had the demands nicely printed out in great detail on many pages. When they were done, Marv presented what he was willing to offer, which fit on one short page. The heads of development met among themselves and after a very short period of time came back to Marv with their reply—meet our demands or we're leaving.

I had so much to learn from people like Marty and Marv, and I was completely open to the process. I would have thought that the next step was to figure out who we couldn't live without and bite the bullet. That is not what happened. Marv spent a few minutes relaxing quietly, got up from his chair, and motioned me to walk with him. He left the meeting room and called together the entire development team right then and there in the open cubicle area. He explained that the top tier of their management had just resigned and anyone who wanted to go with them should make that decision at this time. Those who wished to stay would not be guaranteed a job, but over the next few weeks we would work together to see who was needed to keep the core development going. And that was that. Marv left a few of his people in charge of sorting out the exodus, and we left.

The only thing Marv ever said to me about the whole affair was that if you let people hold you hostage, they will force you to make terrible decisions, and you will lose. You might as well take your bumps up front and at least be in control of your destiny. Who would have believed that just a few months later, one of Marty's senior executives would move the development of the website to New York and relaunch it with a team of less than forty developers. That new website became the foundation for WebMD's entire future.

Again and again I was seeing that each of these intensely challenging business experiences was very beneficial for my spiritual growth. I just kept letting go of whatever discomfort got stirred up within me, and inevitably, a stronger flow of spiritual energy took its place. This growing strength helped prepare me for life's next growth experience: what happened when Marv's reorganization team finally got around to taking aim at my division.

Medical Manager Practice Services Division, as we were known at the time, was one of the largest divisions in WebMD. We had grown to almost two thousand employees, and that made us very ripe for cost cutting. With that in mind, Marv brought the reorganization team down to Alachua for two days of meetings. The first day was devoted to presenting our business plan and vision for the future. Fortunately, we were well prepared to take Marv through our current products with their highly successful revenue generation, as well as the products and services we were working on for the future. It certainly didn't hurt when Sabrina was able to present the tremendous growth of Medical Manager Network Services from a few hundred thousand dollars a year to a fifty-million-dollar-a-year business in just over three years.

It was during these presentations that it really hit me what had happened. John Kang and I had set out to be sure that Medical Manager was not left behind by the enormous potential of Internet companies like Healtheon and WebMD. At the same time, Sabrina and I had been struggling to find a way to get Envoy, or some other clearinghouse, to evolve enough to be able to fulfill our vision for Network

Services. Despite all the negative issues we were facing, the amazing reality was that when the smoke had cleared, we ended up owning all three of these companies—WebMD, Healtheon, and Envoy. Just a short time ago, no one could have even imagined how such a thing could ever take place. It was like so much else I had experienced; the unimaginable had actually happened.

The presentations to Marv and his team went very well. There was palpable excitement in the room throughout the day. Nonetheless, when I returned later that evening, I was shocked to see what had happened to the meeting room. Stretched around the walls of the room were computer printouts with the names of all the Medical Manager Practice Services Division's two thousand employees. Hanging like wallpaper, they foreshadowed the day planned for tomorrow: every name on the list would need to be justified. I was aghast, especially since we had recently requested additional employees to keep up with our growth.

Returning home that evening, I was very concerned about the fate of my employees. Tomorrow could turn out to be a very ugly day. At the same time, I knew that Marv had to cut costs, and it was my job as a corporate executive to help him. This could have created a lot of inner tension, but I decided to just surrender to the reality of the situation and be open to balancing these two areas of concern. I came to peace that night knowing my heart was in the right place, and when tomorrow came, I would do the best I could.

The next morning when I entered the room, I was again shocked by what I saw. The printouts had been taken down, and the walls were back to normal. Before I could inquire what was going on, Marv's second in command walked me out to the hall. He told me that he and Marv had met last night, and the decision was made to skip the "bloodletting" and allow us to continue the fine work we were doing. He told me they were very impressed with what we had achieved and with our plans for the future. As they saw no need for the second day of meetings, Marv had taken an early flight out. His team packed up, shook our hands, and went on their way. I have no idea to this day if the rest of my management team ever saw the ominous sight of those wallpapered walls.

I realized just how extraordinary these events were when a few hours later I received a call from the head of HR at corporate headquarters in New Jersey. He was completely beside himself. He playfully asked me what I had used to drug Marv while he was down here in Alachua. He went on to say that he doubted that such an event had ever taken place in the annals of corporate history. We were all well aware that Marv's purpose in life was to cut costs. That he would come down here with that intention, and simply walk away, is a tribute to both the quality of our division and to Marv as a manager. Medical Manager and I received a number of tributes in 2000, but none was more meaningful to me than receiving such a vote of confidence from someone I respected so much.

49

Hanging Out in
Washington

The year 2000 not only ushered in a new millennium, it brought with it a flurry of recognition for the pinnacle of success that The Medical Manager had achieved. To me, who was just on the magic carpet for the ride, it was all simply a tribute to the perfection of life's flow. I had not sought any recognition; I had just thrown myself into life's wind to see where it would take me.

I was invited by one of our previous board members, Ray Kurzweil, to join him at the White House in March where he was to receive the National Medal of Honor in Technology. Ray is credited with many major inventions, including the first microchip that allowed an electronic keyboard to sound like a grand piano and other real instruments. He is also considered one of the fathers of speech recognition software. Ray had been on Medical Manager Corporation's board, and I had sat on Kurzweil Education System's board. Through it all we had become good friends. He even stayed with us at the Temple a few times and showed a serious interest in Eastern philosophy. I would have to wear a tuxedo to the While House, which was far from my normal attire, but I was excited about joining Ray for this honor.

Like many others, I had been to the White House as a tourist but certainly not as a guest of the president. There was a cocktail party after the ceremony, and we were allowed to walk freely throughout the rooms of the first floor residence. I gazed out a window in the Green Room that overlooked the Washington Monument and thought about how many presidents had taken in that view. Getting used to actually sitting on the antique furniture in those rooms was difficult enough, but then I kept realizing that the people I was having conversations with were all National Medal of Honor winners in some field of science. President Clinton joined the mix, and I even ran into Stevie Wonder in the hallway. All in all, it was one of those "what am I doing here" moments. I'm a yogi who moved out to the woods to meditate. I surrendered to the flow of life, and I end up here—unbelievable.

That was not my only trip to Washington that year. The very next month I came back to represent The Medical Manager when it was installed into the archives of the Smithsonian Institution. The Smithsonian was sponsoring an effort to document the Information Technology Revolution for future generations. In much the same way as we now look at the Industrial Revolution, someday people will be fascinated by the time period in which computers revolutionized how we live. Each year a panel of CEOs of the world's leading IT companies did a search for organizations that had done extraordinary work in the field. Because of our work in the area of electronic health-care transactions, Medical Manager was one of the companies selected in the year 2000 to have its story preserved in a time capsule for the future. There was a grand banquet the night before and a ceremony at the museum the next day. I brought a few of the old-time employees with me, as well as Donna and Durga. Reflecting back twenty years to when I was sitting in that twelve-by-twelve-foot room in the woods by myself writing this program, one could never have imagined that it would lead to the Smithsonian.

As it turned out, I would have to return to DC once again in August of 2000 on a very important trip. I had been asked to represent the company at a meeting with the Department of Justice (DOJ). Before larger companies can combine, the U.S. government reserves the right to determine if the combination could stifle competition and violate antitrust laws. In the case of the Healtheon/WebMD–Medical Manager merger, the government requested very detailed information and a face-to-face meeting. The reason for this was that Medical

Manager Network Services was sending so many claims to Envoy that the government was concerned about allowing us to become part of the same company. My immediate reaction to this situation was one of deep humility. Had Medical Manager actually reached the point of success that the U.S. government had to be concerned about the very antitrust laws I had studied in business school? No, not really, but we were going to have to convince them of that.

Sabrina and I flew up to Washington to prepare for the Justice Department meeting. It was around that time I began to notice that my life was becoming filled with more and more attorneys. We met for a strategy meeting at the office of one of the largest law firms in D.C. There were attorneys everywhere, but one always stood out from the rest. Jim Mercer was Marty's litigation specialist, and he understood both the law and business at a phenomenal level. I had learned to have great respect and confidence in Jim, and I was glad he would be present at the DOJ meeting.

I, of course, had never previously dealt with the Justice Department. It was not exactly my everyday experience to be entering the DOJ building surrounded by a large team of attorneys. Nevertheless, after hours of very intense questioning, Sabrina and I managed to address the government's concerns satisfactorily. When it was all said and done, the merger was not going to pose any anti-trust problems. Though we were very relieved when the ordeal was over, it had actually turned out to be quite a learning experience.

All this exposure to intensely powerful people and situations was having a profound effect on the psyche I watched so diligently. I had never been exposed to this powerful lifestyle. Nothing in me got off on it or wanted anything from it, but it did make me deal with parts of my being that I would not have faced otherwise. If I saw any weakness, fear, or anxiety come up, I just deeply relaxed back into where I was watching from. I simply kept letting go of whatever came up. This is where life had taken me, and I used all these situations as a way of letting go of myself. It was definitely working. I kept being pushed into strongly positive and negative situations, and I increasingly found myself in a very clear and undisturbed state. It seemed that the more challenges life put me through, the less my inner energy flow was affected by outer conditions. What years of willful meditation had not gotten rid of, life's situations and challenges were rooting out of me. As long as I made getting rid of myself my only goal, every situation was a fruitful experience. If I'd had any other goal, I think the constant pressure would have been overwhelming. I found that I actually got more peaceful inside as I dealt with the ever-increasing magnitude of challenges. Life was molding me each day to become who I needed to be in order to handle tomorrow's tasks. All I had to do was let go and not resist the process.

For the next few years, my Medical Manager Practice Services Division continued to grow to its peak financial success. We grew to more than twenty-three hundred employees and were generating more than three hundred million dollars a year in revenue. We were the most widely installed practice management vendor in the country, and we had begun turning our attention toward building a fully computerized electronic health record. It was a period with tremendous challenges that I thought was putting me through unprecedented growth. Little did I know that life's portal of dramatic change was about to open up once again. When it did this time, it would completely redefine for me what it meant to go through a transformational growth experience.

Section IX

. . . .

Total Surrender

50.

The Raid

It was Wednesday, September 3, 2003. I remember because on Wednesdays I go into Gainesville in the morning to see Dr. Chance for a health tune-up. After the appointment, I noticed I had a voice mail from Lisa Elliot, the resident attorney at the R&D facility in Alachua. She said it was very important, so I returned her call while still in the parking lot. I got Lisa on her cell phone, and she was very glad to hear from me. Her voice was uncharacteristically tense, and I realized that something was very wrong. She began by telling me that I needed to come to work right away because the FBI was there, and they wanted to see me. My first thought was about a federal marshal who had come to the facility a few years earlier looking for a prior employee. I asked Lisa if they were looking for someone. She said, "No, THE FBI is here—twelve to fifteen agents plus the Sheriff's Department. They've taken over the entire facility. They've shut down all the phone lines and the entire computer system. This is a full-blown raid. Helicopters are flying overhead, agents are armed, and there's a search warrant. You need to come here right away!"

I clearly heard the words she was saying, and I understood the sense of urgency with which they were said—but the situation was so absurd that I could not relate to it in any manner. It was like—maybe they have the wrong address. I guess that's why it didn't disturb me. In fact, it sounded like it was going to be rather exciting getting to show them they had made a mistake. I asked Lisa what was going on. Why were they there? She said she had no idea, but apparently the same thing was happening at our offices in Tampa and at corporate headquarters in New Jersey. She had been trying to call Charlie Mele, our general counsel, but she couldn't get through. The phones were down corporatewide. I assured her that I would be there right away.

During the twenty-minute drive back to the office, I tried calling everyone I could think of who might have some information. I still had absolutely no idea what was going on when I pulled up to the R&D facility. The front drive was completely blocked off with Sheriff's Department vehicles, and the employees showing up for work were being turned away. I pulled up to a deputy and identified myself. He made a call on his radio and immediately signaled to the others to let me through. As I drove up the long and winding drive through the beautiful hayfields, law enforcement vehicles were scattered everywhere. When I approached Building 1, I saw the Sheriff's Department's forty-foot Mobile Command Center stretched across our parking lot. We had five buildings by then, and FBI and Sheriff's Department personnel were positioned around all of them. There were, indeed, two helicopters buzzing overhead. I think they ended up being part of the media coverage.

I parked in my normal spot and made my way into the building. The place was swarming with law enforcement officers. I was met by four or five agents who immediately walked me into the back conference room where I was to spend the day. I requested that our in-house attorney, Lisa, be present, and she was brought into the room. The agents identified themselves as from the FBI and Treasury Department. They were very professional and businesslike. I was presented with a search warrant, which Lisa had already reviewed, and I was informed that the warrant gave them full control of the facility. They had the right to take any and all items that fell within the itemized categories. They asked me to sign a paper acknowledging that I had been served the warrant. I glanced at Lisa, and she nodded that I should sign. I had absolutely no idea what to do; I was completely out of my element. The only frame of reference I had for this sort of thing was the movies, and I doubted that was going to be of much help.

I asked the agents in charge if they could help me understand what was going on. They didn't say much, but they referred me to a list of about thirty names that they said were persons essential to their investigation. The entire executive management team from the original Medical Manager Corporation was on the list, as were Marty, the attorney Jim Mercer, and some top people from WebMD's corporate accounting. My mouth must have been agape as I looked at the list. But there were also a few other names that really floored me, like the senior auditor from the highly respected public accounting firm we had used for Medical Manager Corporation. I was taking everything in very calmly, but my mind was spinning trying to find clues about what was behind all of this.

It was actually the presence of one name on the list that first caught my attention. The name was Pat Sedlacek. Unlike everyone else on the list, this person was neither part of our executive team nor part of legal or accounting. Pat worked on the dealer acquisition team, which was run by Bobby Davids, our VP of acquisitions. Bobby had come into the company at the time of the 1997 initial public offering, along with John Sessions, our chief operations officer; and David Ward, our VP of sales. I would hardly have recognized Pat's name out of our twenty-three hundred division employees, except that we were currently in the process of investigating him for taking kickbacks from some of the dealers. That investigation had begun in late 2002 and by early 2003 had included Bobby Davids and a couple of other employees. WebMD's corporate attorneys, with the help of outside counsel, were handling the matter. We had already fired the people involved and sued them in a Tampa court in order to obtain subpoena power and freeze Bobby's and Pat's assets.

As our investigation went on, we were finding more and more incidents of Bobby and/or Pat arranging kickbacks from the dealers they were acquiring. The subpoenas we obtained of their bank accounts had revealed an intricate network of shell companies Bobby had been using to hide the money. The investigators were able to trace the funds coming in and going out of these accounts to see who was involved in the money trail. Pat had already begun to cooperate, and it was obvious that Bobby Davids was the ringleader. By the time of the raid, we had traced millions of dollars, and it was still an ongoing investigation. With both Pat's and Bobby's names on the list, and the search warrant listing more than a hundred of our dealer acquisitions, it was likely that these raids were somehow related to what Bobby had been doing. But his kickback schemes involved only four or five employees, and our investigation of the matter was being dealt with in the open. Why couldn't the government just talk to the investigating attorneys? Why a sneak-attack raid in Alachua, Tampa, and New Jersey when everything was readily available?

I was finally able to get Charlie, WebMD's general counsel, on my cell phone. He confirmed that they had been raided by the FBI at WebMD's headquarters in New Jersey, and he was as much in the dark as I was. He also suspected that this might be associated with the illegal activity Bobby Davids had been involved in. We discussed the possibility that Bobby had tried to strike a deal by telling the government that all the executives were involved in his kickbacks. If so, it didn't seem likely that his story would hold up given all the hard evidence we had of his bank accounts and cancelled checks. Charlie said that we would get more clarification over the next few days; in the meantime, we were to cooperate fully with the agents.

A sense of total peace came over me and pretty much remained there the entire day. It was so thick it felt like a protective blanket. I was not concerned in the least. I knew I had not done anything wrong, and therefore they were not going to find anything. If this was a case of Bobby lying to try to save his neck, the evidence would clearly reveal the truth. I wanted to make sure I was present enough to fully take in this extraordinary experience. It's not every day that the FBI shows up and raids your place for absolutely no apparent reason.

My understanding is that nationwide more than fifty government agents were involved in the raid. They took the entire day, and by the time they were done, they left with pretty much everything. My desk was cleared of every single scrap of paper. All my file cabinets were empty, as were all those of my executive assistant, Sandy Plumb. All legal files were removed from Lisa's office and from the legal filing rooms. My conference room table used to have stacks of file folders piled up that were actively being used to run the business. They were all gone with no way to re-create them. And it was not just the paper documents that were being taken; agents were also making mirror images of all our computer disk drives, both the desktops and the servers.

The day progressed pretty much without my input. I used my time to work on remaining completely comfortable with the radical situation life had stuck me in. There was really no reason to be thinking about why this was happening or how it would turn out. Since I had absolutely no idea what was going on, thinking about it wasn't going to help. Instead, I enjoyed spending my day letting go of whatever that voice in my head was trying to say and deeply relaxing whenever my heart began to feel anxious. In this situation, surrender was not an option; it was only sane thing to do.

When I left that evening, I sought out the lead agents. I thanked them for being so cordial and told them that I wished we could have met under better circumstances. To me, they were just people doing their jobs to the best of their ability—it certainly wasn't their fault.

When the sun set on September 3, 2003, nationwide, the government had taken 1.2 million e-mail messages, 1,500 boxes of files containing more than 3 million pages of documents, and 830,000 computer files. This was, indeed, a day that would live in infamy.

51

Attorneys, Attorneys, and More Attorneys

The next morning I got a preview of what my life was going to be like for a while. The headlines of the *Gainesville Sun* read, "FBI Raids Alachua Medical Manager Offices." Underneath was my picture next to the story heading, "Wall Street Halts the Trading of WebMD Stock Just Before Noon." I knew it didn't make any difference that I hadn't done anything and that I didn't even know what the raid was all about—I was headline news. I had never been publicly disgraced before, and I noticed that it definitely stirred up the psyche. That voice inside my head kept wanting to explain that this had nothing to do with me. There was certainly no lack of people wanting to hear what I had to say. Media outlets from all over the country, including the *Wall Street Journal* and *New York Times*, were trying to reach me for a comment.

Fortunately, I knew better. I had spent all these years quieting down that mental voice, and I had learned that listening to it only fuels the fire. I knew how powerful it was to simply relax and release past that urge to defend oneself. I resolved to only discuss the matter when absolutely necessary. Otherwise, I would just go about my business as usual. I hadn't done anything wrong, so why should I let this affect me? Over time it would work itself out. In the meantime, I was not going to let it steal the great peace and joy I felt deep inside. Right from the beginning, I resolved to use the whole situation to finally free myself from whatever was left of that scared person inside who

had always held me back. This was my entire journey—liberation at
any cost.

We had a conference call with the corporate attorneys first thing
in the morning. No one could make sense of what had happened. Regardless, the first order of business was to hire an attorney. Well, not
exactly *an* attorney—separate law firms to represent both the company and the board of directors, and a criminal attorney for everyone
whose name was on the list. I could see that the corporate attorneys
were taking this very seriously. They explained that it didn't matter if
you were as clean as a whistle; a raid of this magnitude foreshadowed
major problems, and everyone needed legal representation. That meant
at least twenty attorneys. I soon found out even that wasn't going to be
enough. The investigation was coming out of the U.S. Attorney's Office in Charleston, South Carolina, so it was suggested that the senior
executives also line up attorneys licensed to practice there. So now we
were talking about hiring thirty to forty attorneys, plus two firms for
the company. If I hadn't been stunned by the raid, I was certainly going
to be stunned by what it meant to defend yourself against it.

I couldn't relate to suddenly being thrust into this situation. I knew
absolutely nothing about criminal matters; I had never even thought
about the subject. This made me very naive about the inherent danger
I could be facing. If I had been left on my own, I probably would have
figured that since I didn't do anything, I should just go in and talk
to the government. Fortunately, I was surrounded by savvy businesspeople who knew that you don't do anything until you consult an attorney and find out what's going on. I certainly learned the wisdom of
that advice as events unfolded.

Over the next few weeks, WebMD's board hired Williams and
Connolly to represent the company. This firm was not the largest in
Washington, but it had the reputation of being one of the best for this
sort of case. I asked Jim Mercer, since he was the attorney I respected
the most, to help me select my attorney. I was a novice and he was an
expert. I really appreciated all the help and support I got from him. Jim
steered me to an attorney at Williams and Connolly who gave me a list

of highly respected criminal lawyers whom he had worked with in the past. It seemed like such a big decision. I wouldn't have any idea how to interview a top-notch criminal attorney. I followed Jim's advice and started to set up preliminary meetings with some of the attorneys—but in my heart, I knew I was going to leave this decision up to the flow of life.

As it turned out, events unfolded such that I met with only one attorney, Randy Turk. Randy was a senior partner with Baker Botts, one of the country's oldest and most respected law firms. His résumé read like a Who's Who in the white-collar criminal defense world. It ran from successfully defending Hughes Aircraft Company against a $400 million claim by the U.S. government regarding repair of the Hubble space telescope, to being one of the key lawyers on the defense team for Michael K. Deaver, Reagan White House deputy chief of staff, at a trial of allegations of perjury and obstruction of justice. The list went on and on.

Of all the information I could gather about Randy, it was something the attorney at Williams and Connolly said that influenced me the most. He had heard that I had a ponytail and lived in the woods. He told me that of all the top defense attorneys he knew, Randy was the most avant-garde. The attorney felt that based on what he had heard about me, Randy and I would get along great.

I met Randy for the first time in New York. He flew in for the WebMD shareholder meeting to meet with me and Jim Mercer, who was helping me select my attorney. I was immediately comfortable with Randy. He had been defending people against government charges for more than thirty years. He practiced in Washington and was obviously very successful. Randy seemed to be intrigued by the case and my unique background. He had learned what he could from his contact at Williams and Connolly, and Jim and I proceeded to tell him what we knew.

WebMD had gotten a much better idea of the focus of the government's investigation by the time Randy and I met. As we had suspected, Bobby Davids was behind all of this. After the company had successfully subpoenaed his hidden bank accounts in early 2003, Bobby knew he was caught. It was just a matter of time before we realized that he had stolen almost six million dollars in kickbacks and embezzlement schemes. He was going to prison for a very long time. But Bobby was a con man, and apparently a very good one. He had certainly conned us for years while managing to carry out his fraud undetected. In March 2003, Bobby Davids embarked on the con of his life—how to avoid punishment for what he had done. He walked into the U.S. Attorney's Office in Charleston, South Carolina, near where he lived, and presented himself as a whistle-blower. He told the federal authorities that he was an executive who had been involved in massive accounting fraud at a public company. He admitted that as part of this fraud he had taken kickbacks for himself and a few others, but he was prepared to turn in the entire upper management team if the government was prepared to cut him a deal.

For the next six months leading up to the raid, while WebMD attorneys were openly investigating all that Davids and his group had done, Bobby Davids was secretly hand-feeding the government an intricate web of lies. Davids was, in fact, a CPA in charge of the entire dealer acquisition program. As such, he had detailed knowledge of every acquisition and every supporting document. Davids was completely free to create the entire frame of reference for the government about the company and its executives. With the skill of a Picasso, he was painting a masterpiece on the blank canvas of people's minds. All he had to do was be sure he told the story in a way that would later be supportable by the documents they would find. He knew there was not going to be any hard evidence found to support his "world according to Bobby." But if he says that he was told to do a deal in a certain way, and he could later show that, indeed, the deal was done that way— that would support his story. The problem is that it would not support the "he was told" part. But if he tells the government investigators what they're going to find, and they keep finding it, that would lend credence to the rest of his story. Eventually, he would earn their confidence. If knowledge is power, then Bobby Davids had all the power.

In that early interaction with the government, he was the one with all the knowledge.

Randy explained that this was not an unusual situation. The government forms a view and then tries to find evidence to support that view. That is what the FBI was currently doing with the mass of documents taken during the raid. Randy said the problem with that many documents is that you can always find a way to make them say what you want. On that ominous note, Randy agreed to defend me to the best of his ability, and we shook hands. I could never have known the odyssey we were about to embark on together. Nor could I have known how close our friendship would become. All I knew at the time was that the same flow of life's events that had led me into this mess had just led me to my lead attorney. Following this flow was my great experiment, and there was no turning back now.

52.

United States of America v. Michael A. Singer

Four months had passed since the raid, and we still knew very little about what was going on. I continued to feel confident that as the government investigators worked their way through the documents and interviewed people in the company, they would realize that Bobby and his group were the only ones who had done anything wrong. The headlines had stopped, and everything was relatively back to normal in our daily lives. Randy came down to Alachua once or twice, as did a few members of his team. Since we didn't know what case the government was trying to build, and they had taken all the documents from 1997 through 2003, there was not much legal work we could be doing. The only thing the executives could do was start getting our attorneys up to speed regarding our business and personal histories.

Randy selected a South Carolina attorney for me, John Simmons, and shortly thereafter John came down to see me. I was very impressed with him. John had been the U.S. attorney for South Carolina in the past and was now in private practice. As we spent the day together, and he saw what I had built over the years with the business and the Temple, he grew more and more dismayed at what was going on. He told me he knew the prosecutor leading the investigation, and she was a fine, intelligent woman. Like everyone else involved, John wondered how Bobby had managed to pull her into his world.

Randy told me that these large, white-collar investigations were measured in years, not months. He said there wasn't much for us to do until the government investigators had worked through what they had seized and were prepared to discuss their case. He did say that we could contact the prosecutor to inquire about my status on the list. I was shocked to learn I was one of the chief targets of the investigation. This did not surprise Randy. The government was head-hunting, and because I had been the CEO, that put me on the top of the list. Regardless, I continued to believe that since they weren't going to find anything, I had nothing to worry about. I believed that in the end, truth would triumph.

In the meantime, the company moved forward aggressively with its defense. A firm was hired to finish off the internal investigation of Bobby's kickback schemes. Just because he had somehow managed to get the government on his side didn't mean that he hadn't stolen from the company. In addition, the company set out to show that it was not true that there was rampant accounting fraud going on in the company. The board hired a forensic accounting firm to perform a detailed audit of revenue and earnings of the Medical Manager Practice Services Division for the entire year of 2001. As a public company, it was very important to protect WebMD from getting pulled into this mess. Fortunately, they were successful.

As part of isolating the company from the investigation of the individual Medical Manager executives, in July 2004, I stepped down as CEO of the division. Later that year, as the investigation heated up, I also stepped down from WebMD's board of directors. I saw this as another act of surrender of the personal in order to serve what life was doing. I just relaxed and let go of whatever resistance came up inside of me. That is how I had been handling this entire ordeal, and it made that period of my life a profound and powerful part of my spiritual journey.

January 2005 brought the next major step in the process. The government accepted plea agreements from Bobby Davids and two of his collaborators in the kickback schemes. These people agreed to pay restitutions to the company, and Bobby agreed to serve a year and a day in prison. Not bad, considering when it was all said and done he admitted to stealing $5.4 million in fifty-three kickback schemes over a five-year period. The only charge Bobby Davids and the others faced was one count of mail fraud.

The rest of us were pretty much beside ourselves. It didn't bode well for us that the government was willing to let these people off so lightly in exchange for their testimony against us. We had also found that Bobby had been having an affair with a woman in the accounting department. She was a CPA and the comptroller for the dealer acquisitions program. To a large part, it was her cooperation that allowed Bobby to get his schemes past accounting, the auditors, and the executives. Yet she was not charged at all. It was at that point that I started to realize just how much the cards were stacked against us. The government was letting admittedly guilty people go in order to get their testimony. These people were just pointing up the ladder to get the spotlight off themselves. Regardless, the story in the papers read that some Medical Manager executives had pleaded guilty to being involved in accounting fraud, and more people were likely to be charged. The whole thing was a PR nightmare for WebMD and the Medical Manager Practice Services Division. The last thing in the world I wanted to do was hurt the company. After twenty-five years of committed service, it was time to resign. On February 9, 2005, I sent my resignation letter to WebMD's CEO. It may well be the only resignation letter written under these circumstances that was ever signed, "With great love and respect." I meant every word of it.

I was amazed that after all those years my inner state was not affected by leaving the company. I woke up the next morning, went to the Temple as I always did, then walked up to the old Personalized Programming office building on Temple grounds. That building had been converted into a house, but no one was living there. My old office had been used as a study, and it still had the same desk and furniture as fifteen years earlier. I found that I was just as comfortable with this office as I was with the executive suite down the road. In fact, I was more comfortable. I had always liked simplicity; that's why I had moved out to the woods in the first place. Sitting quietly in that office, I could see that this terrible situation was bringing about amazing changes—both inside and out. Life had always done that to me, and accepting those changes was my great experiment. I knew that this attack by the government was no exception. I just had to be willing to go wherever it took me.

In the meantime, I had been given the space to begin writing the books I always knew I was going to write. There were two of them: The first would impart what I had learned since first noticing my mental voice talking while I was sitting on that couch so many years ago. It would be a journey back to the seat of Self that could be taken by anyone in the world. It was to be called *The Untethered Soul*. The second book would be the stories of the miraculous flow of events that happened over the years as I let go and let life unfold naturally. It would be called *The Surrender Experiment*. I couldn't start that book yet, because I had no idea how this latest chapter would play out. So in the midst of all this change and uncertainty, I began working on *The Untethered Soul*.

Karen Entner had lived at the Temple for more than fifteen years. She had grown into a management position at Medical Manager where she was a phenomenally productive employee. As head of the documentation and computer-based training departments, she had been writing under my supervision for years. Shortly after I left the company, she expressed an interest in helping with my book. So now I had a book to write and the perfect person to assist with the process. The Temple, the book, and periodic conversations with Randy and his team kept me plenty busy for the rest of the year.

By November 2005, a full two years after the raid, Randy was hearing that an indictment was imminent. He and some of the other attorneys demanded to see evidence tying their clients to a crime. The result was that Randy sent me a one-inch-thick stack of documents that the government intended to use to prove I was behind Bobby's activities.

I was very interested in getting to study this material, yet at the same time I was somewhat apprehensive. After only a few hours, I was flabbergasted. I did not see anything in these documents that incriminated me. There were some accounting reports on a few acquisitions Bobby had done, but most of the rest were handwritten notes my assistant, Sandy, had taken during our twice weekly executive calls. On these notes, the FBI had circled pretty much every reference to any discussions we had about meeting our quarterly revenue and earnings projections. Sandy had scribbled my name next to some of the comments or suggestions. That was about it. I was both relieved and concerned. I was relieved because, as I suspected, they didn't find anything indicating I had done anything wrong. I felt concerned because they were obviously considering these circled documents as evidence against me. I didn't know what to think, so I called Randy.

Randy told me that everyone who had looked at the documents had the same reaction—there was nothing in them that tied me to any wrongdoing. Randy explained that it didn't matter. Bobby had said that the accounting fraud he had been involved in was for the purpose of meeting Wall Street's numbers. These documents would be used to show motive. The government prosecutors would argue that since I wanted to meet Wall Street's expectations, I allowed Bobby to do things improperly. Motive was one of the pieces the government needed in order to try to build a case against me. But this wasn't just happening to me. Randy told me that every one of the other executives, and their attorneys, had the same reaction to the materials they were given.

Just one month later, on December 19, 2005, Randy received notification from the U.S. Marshals Office in Columbia, South Carolina, that a federal indictment had been issued—I was under arrest. Along with nine other prior executives of Medical Manager Corporation, I was to turn myself in to the federal authorities at an arraignment on December 28 in Charleston, South Carolina. The summons read:

UNITED STATES OF AMERICA V.
MICHAEL A. SINGER

53

Preparing a Defense

I thought I pretty much understood what I was up against until I saw the indictment. In all honesty, it was about the furthest thing from the truth that I had ever seen in my life. I knew that Bobby had implicated us by telling the government that we were aware of everything he had done wrong. In the eyes of the law, that would have made us co-conspirators. But the indictment did not even include Bobby Davids's name. It listed all the things he claimed to have done improperly and stated that the executives did these things—or more precisely, "caused them to happen." We were all facing conspiracy charges that could result in up to fifteen years in prison.

I was floored when I first read the indictment. Randy was not. It was just about what he had expected based on his thirty years of experience. The indictment represented the government's story in the strongest possible language to justify the charges. Truth, on the other hand, could hopefully emerge from the fires of the trial. So far there had been absolutely no pushback against Bobby's view of the world. We had, in fact, not yet begun to fight.

I met Randy and my South Carolina attorney, John Simmons, in Charleston for the arraignment. All ten of the indicted Medical Manager executives were there, along with more than twenty of our attorneys. Joining me were John Kang, John Sessions, Rick Karl, David Ward, two regional vice presidents, the chief financial officer, an accounting comptroller, and the attorney who had worked on the dealer acquisition program. It was quite a circus. Before the court proceedings, we all had to get booked and fingerprinted by the FBI. Needless to say, that was a first-time experience for all of us.

When we were finally brought together outside the courtroom, it was the first time many of us had seen each other for years. We had built a successful company together and there was still real friendship and camaraderie between us. The attorneys preferred that we not speak to one another, but that just wasn't going to happen. The scene turned into a reunion with warm handshakes and hugs. Each of us knew in our hearts that we had not done the things we were being accused of. Perhaps the sense of a common enemy brought us even closer together. All I know is that by the time the prosecutor showed up, it looked more like a social gathering than an arraignment.

I really wanted to meet the prosecutor. I didn't hold anything against her. In fact, I felt a strange kinship with her because we both had been duped by the same con artist—Bobby Davids. The difference being that I knew it and she didn't. Against Randy's better judgment, but with his permission, I introduced myself to her. She shook my hand, but it was very clear that she didn't like me very much. It was the first time we had ever met, but she had already built a Mickey Singer inside her head who I'm sure I'd rather not meet.

The proceedings progressed smoothly except that instead of one defendant and his attorney standing before the judge, we had to squeeze in ten defendants and twenty attorneys. The courtroom was quite small, and the public seating area was completely filled with the remainder of our legal teams. The room was so packed that the jury box was being used to hold ten to twelve inmates in orange jumpsuits who were waiting their turn to see the judge. I was standing right next to the jury box, and these inmates reminded me of my group back in prison. I allowed myself to think that the way things were going—that could be me someday. I knew if I was going to be at peace throughout this ordeal, I would have to be comfortable with that thought. I just let go and relaxed into the moment. I was standing in a South Carolina courtroom being arraigned, but I was overcome with love for those inmates sitting next to me. Randy had to nudge me to stand up straight and pay attention to the proceedings. All I knew was that I was on the journey of my life and just look where it had taken me.

The judge released us on our own recognizance without the need to post bail. Though we were free to leave, I lingered in that courtroom for a while and wondered what it had in store for me. These were very unique moments in one's life—best not to miss them.

I spent time with some of the executives afterward. I hadn't seen Rick Karl for many years, but that hadn't affected our close friendship. He told me he had been nominated for a federal judgeship in Florida. Indications were that he would have received the appointment, but he had to pull his name the moment he heard he had been indicted. Likewise, John Kang was preparing to step down as chairman and CEO of the public company he and his brother had started. Everyone was putting their best face forward, but this situation was altering people's lives.

Aside from these executives and their families, the front-page publicity from the indictment had affected some other people very dear to me. I had already received a call from the warden at Union Correctional Institution saying that until this situation was resolved, he had no choice but to revoke my authorization to meet with my Saturday morning group. After thirty years of committing myself to perhaps the most important thing I had done in my life, my prison work was over. A wave of darkness was falling over everything that had been the source of so much light. It was all completely out of my control. I was determined to sit peacefully deep inside and see if it could pass by without affecting my inner state. It was like the early days when I had first started my experiment of letting go in the face of perceived danger. The big difference now was that this danger was way beyond anything I could have ever imagined. It was the perfect storm.

Meanwhile, it had been over two years since the raid. The government was required by law to disclose all the materials investigators had seized. Yet by the time of the arraignment, we still had no documents with which to prepare a defense. That evening, the entire joint defense group got together at a hotel. I really enjoyed watching all the attorneys interact. Randy had taken the lead in putting together a joint defense agreement that would allow us to share materials. But in the end, each attorney was responsible for their own client's best interest. Surrounded by a roomful of criminal defense attorneys, I realized that I was in an amazing situation. I was about to embark on a very personal tour of the American justice system. I knew I had never even thought of doing the things I was accused of. But how was this going to turn out? Would our great system of justice work?

A month later we began to receive the first wave of disclosure materials. We gained access to the 1.2 million e-mail messages taken during the raid as well as the notes from some of the FBI interviews. It would be five more months before we had any access to the millions of pages of paper documents that had been seized, not to mention the hundreds of thousands of computer files that had been copied during the raid. The government had almost three years to review all this material; it was going to take the defense years to work through it.

Once the disclosure materials began arriving, Randy and the Baker Botts team kept giving me tasks to do: review these tens of thousands of e-mail messages; review all six years of notes from the executive meetings; review all my written responses to years of nightly take-home work. I would periodically go up to D.C. to work with the team on specific items. There were always four or five attorneys from Baker Botts working on the case on my behalf. All the other executives' attorneys also had dedicated teams, though not always as large. The further we got into the material, the more obvious it became—no one except Bobby and his group had done anything wrong. There were no e-mail messages or documents that showed any executive instructing, or even implying, that accounting should be done improperly. We had thirty to forty of our attorneys buried in these documents solely to find anything that could tie us to Bobby's misdeeds. No one found any hard evidence against any of the defendants. Unfortunately, since we had worked with Bobby Davids on a regular basis, there would always be circumstantial evidence that could be exploited to mean whatever you wanted it to mean.

This was the backdrop under which I wrote *The Untethered Soul*. To the core of my being, I wanted to communicate to others that they were deep inside listening to that voice's incessant chatter, and there was a way they could be free. That was the work of my life—not this absurd legal mess. I didn't care how threatening this nontruth had become—I wanted to share a deep truth that would brighten the lives of others. I committed myself to the book. Karen and I had finished writing by late 2006, but we were still doing editing passes. I sent an early draft to Randy because I wanted to get his feedback. I also needed my attorney's permission to do just about anything that might affect the case. Randy was very concerned that the government prosecutors would find a way to use the book against me, as they had been doing with everything else. I told him that I was willing to take that risk. Especially since we had no idea where the case would end up, I needed to get the book published as soon as possible. Having discussed the risks, Randy left the decision to me.

Getting *The Untethered Soul* published came together very quickly. I had given an early draft to James O'Dea, a dear friend of mine who was on the Temple's board of trustees. As the perfection of life would have it, James was the director of the Institute of Noetic Sciences (IONS) at the time, and they had just signed a co-publishing arrangement with New Harbinger Publications, the country's foremost psychology book publisher. They all read the book and loved it. Given how everything else in my life was being pulled toward the abyss, it amazed me to see these energies flow so smoothly.

The Untethered Soul was launched in September 2007. I bypassed the customary promotional book signing tour and declined all interviews. I knew it was an author's responsibility to promote their book, especially during the launch, so I informed New Harbinger that I would handle the publicity by way of the Internet. Karen and I devised a marketing strategy, and without leaving the woods of Alachua, we poured time and money into promoting the book. The results were phenomenal. New Harbinger's first press run of *The Untethered Soul* was supposed to last a year—we ran out of books in just three months.

The book has continued to sell very well on its own after the launch, including internationally. In the midst of that intensely dark period, the book managed to manifest, sprout wings, and soar off around the globe. The feedback from everywhere was overwhelming. *The Untethered Soul* was fulfilling its purpose—it was helping people. In the midst of phenomenal darkness, it was spreading light.[3]

---

3 Publisher's note: In November 2012, *The Untethered Soul* became a number one *New York Times* bestseller.

54

The Constitution and the Bill of Rights

The legal battle was definitely getting more interesting. Once we had access to the disclosure materials, we could prepare a defense. The first thing Randy and the defense team did was ask the judge to force the government to cut the scope of the materials down to size. They couldn't just hand us millions and millions of e-mail messages, documents, and computer files, as well as years of accounting entries, and then say somewhere in there is what you did wrong. If we were going to have a chance of defending ourselves, the claims of wrongdoing needed to be more specific. In legal terms, this is called requesting a "bill of particulars." The government fought it, but the judge issued an order forcing prosecutors to specify exactly which dealer acquisitions and which accounting entries they were going to present at trial.

In all these years of seeing the truth manipulated until it became unrecognizable, this was the first time I saw that we had some say in the matter. The U.S. Department of Justice is one of the most powerful forces in the world. But it is not all-powerful. The judge had the right to overrule the DOJ. I reminded myself that this was not the case in lots of other countries. If those governments were convinced that you did something wrong, it was pretty much over. As long as I had to go through this ordeal, I wanted to learn all that I could about our legal system. I asked Randy what exactly gave us the right to make this demand of the government. I really loved his answer—the Constitution.

The Sixth Amendment says, "The accused shall enjoy the right . . . to be informed of the nature and cause of the accusations." Supreme Court rulings through the years have interpreted this right to mean that if the disclosure materials presented to you are too broad in scope, you have the right to demand a bill of particulars.

I didn't tell Randy at the time, but that moved me to the core of my being. For three years I had been sitting quietly deep inside myself watching the powers that be take Bobby's lies and turn them into a seemingly unstoppable force of destruction. Suddenly, I was reminded that people I'd never met had possessed the caring and foresight to make sure I had rights. If it was going to be the United States of America versus Michael A. Singer, I had some very great people in my corner—Thomas Jefferson, George Mason, and James Madison, to name just a few. Over the next few years, it would become painfully obvious to me that only a single piece of paper stood between me and the dark abyss. That piece of paper was the U.S. Constitution.

I went back and read the Constitution, beginning to end. From the perspective of my predicament, it was so evident that the Founding Fathers were not only creating a government, they were protecting the people from it. I had always known this intellectually, but now it was personal, very personal. This was not a civics course—it was my life. Under these circumstances the Constitution really came alive for me.

Throughout 2007, the joint defense group worked on finding all relevant documents regarding the items the government had listed on the bill of particulars. I went up to Washington a few days each month for review meetings and also had regular conference calls with the legal team at Baker Botts. Randy was present for almost all the meetings, and his partner, Casey Cooper, and the associate attorneys handled much of the day-to-day work.

Each associate had been assigned a share of the dealer acquisitions to thoroughly reconstruct, and we would review each of these transactions in painstaking detail. It was like having a jackhammer taken to my ego. I had built and run a beautiful company. We had a great product, great employees, and great clients, and we had been very successful. But underneath the dealer acquisition program, there was filth. It was like looking into a cesspool. Bobby had been stealing, lying, manipulating, and controlling everything in his world—including me and the rest of the executives. It took my breath away to see what he had done. Behind it all was the realization that these meetings were not about what Bobby had done; they were about the fact that he had managed to find a way to make us criminally responsible for what he had done. It was like being in the *Twilight Zone*. All I could do was keep letting go at the deepest possible level. My mantra was: This Is Reality—Deal with It. I just took the attitude that on my journey through life, I was now part of this excellent legal team that had been pulled together to defend this poor sap, Singer, who had been framed by the evil villain. I took a breath, let go, and contributed positively to the topic being discussed.

We were definitely making headway. We had discovered that the disk drive the government gave us that held data from people's personal computer files had been indexed improperly by the FBI. For some reason the agents had only indexed the files by the short description header they had assigned to each file. The contents of the files had not been indexed for search purposes. This severely limited the search results of this important source of data. The defense team had a full indexing done, and we were finding lots of interesting historical documents. We found early drafts of documents and letters that directly contradicted some of the lies Bobby had told. Little by little we were unraveling the convoluted mess he had created.

Judge Blatt was our judge, and Randy was doing really well with him. We were having regular pretrial hearings, and Judge Blatt was approving many, but not all, of our motions. Randy found him to be very fair in his rulings and felt that the judge was beginning to get a sense of how far the government had stretched its case. It had been more than four years since the raid, and things were finally beginning to look up. I couldn't have felt more confident in Randy as my lead attorney and as the leading figure in the joint defense group.

Things began to unravel in 2008. Randy informed me on

February 7 that he had gone in for a checkup, and they had found a tumor. It was cancerous and they wanted to operate immediately. They ripped open his chest and cut out the tumor. In the midst of the battle, the general was down.

It only took three or four weeks for Randy to be back on his feet leading the charge. But there was a lingering issue. The doctors said there was a good chance that the tumor could return, and he should consider chemotherapy. He decided to wait and see, hoping for the best. In the meantime, it was back to work. That was a good thing because the government had been petitioning the judge to finally set a trial date. We had been telling the judge that due to the sheer volume of the disclosure materials, we were nowhere near ready. But in June 2008 the judge gave us our trial date—February 2, 2009, just seven months away. We had so much work left to do; it really was going to take an army of attorneys.

Halfway to the trial date, Randy's cancer returned. This time he was going to need eight weeks of very intense chemotherapy and an indeterminate recovery period. I remembered back to when Jim Mercer was advising me about choosing an attorney. He said the Holy Grail would be to get a senior partner from one of the country's premier firms who would be personally committed to your case alone. Randy had turned out to be that Holy Grail. Now, against his doctor's advice, Randy was seriously considering risking his life by waiting until the trial was over before starting his treatment. I assured him I would have none of that, but he decided to wait and see how fast the tumor was progressing before making his decision. Randy was like a Samurai warrior who had finally been given a battle that was about Honor, Truth, and Justice. He was not about to lay down his sword for a tiny tumor.

Unfortunately, it only took a month for the tumor to progress to the point that there was no longer a decision. We knew Judge Blatt was adamant that there would not be any extensions of the trial date. Though it was a long shot, Randy requested a three-month extension so that he could represent me at trial. Once again, it was the Constitution that took care of me. The motion filed invoked my Sixth Amendment right to have the assistance of counsel of my choice. Though the government opposed the motion for an extension, it was granted by the judge under the condition that I begin working with another lead attorney in case Randy did not recover in time. With the new trial date set for May 4, 2009, just five months away, Randy began his treatment.

I had been working with Randy for more than five years by then. He had not only been my lead attorney and good friend, but he was also the chief legal strategist for the entire joint defense group. There was no replacing him. Having promised the judge that I would do just that, at least as a backup, I took a deep breath and surrendered to the reality before me: I would have to start working with a new lead attorney.

55.

Divine Intervention

The workload increased significantly as we moved toward trial. In February, we started a very interesting and important phase of the pretrial hearings—motions *in limine*. These were pretrial motions that gave us the opportunity to challenge whether the evidence the government prosecutors intended to present at trial was, in fact, trustworthy from a legal perspective. They had taken document after document and defined them in a way that seemed to support their version of events. I knew for a fact that many of the documents didn't say what they were being twisted to say. But taken out of context, they would influence a jury. I was pleased to learn that the courts had interpreted our constitutional right to a fair trial to mean that a jury could not be prejudiced with evidence that did not meet a reasonable standard of trustworthiness. In other words, we had the right to petition the judge to exclude some of this material from the trial altogether.

Motion by motion we challenged the relevance and/or trustworthiness of what the government intended to present to the jury. In many cases, the judge agreed with us. This judge was finally reining in the unbridled attempts to create evidence by arbitrarily assigning meaning to documents and events. I was not attending any of the pretrial hearings, but I was reviewing all the motions and following with great interest as they had their day in court. With Randy out, the associate attorney, Alex Walsh, would give me the daily updates. I was really impressed with her and could see how Randy's absence afforded tremendous opportunity for the younger attorneys. I loved seeing that out of this darkness, something great was being forged.

Randy completed his chemotherapy and tried to come back to work right away. But though the therapy was successful, it would take a few months before he got his full strength back. In late March, just one month from trial, we learned that Randy's recovery period was not our only concern. On March 27, 2009, Judge Blatt announced that because of his age and his health, he was stepping down from the case. We had lost our judge.

The saber rattling began immediately. The government sent out word to all defense counsel that they had better come in and negotiate a plea because they were going to be destroyed in trial with a new judge. Needless to say, given how well Judge Blatt had come to know the case over the last three and half years, and how fair he had been, the prospect of a new judge at the eleventh hour was disheartening. In the midst of the most dangerous situation of my life, the two forces in this world I had come to have the most confidence in to protect me, Randy and Judge Blatt, were both taken away. This amazing sequence of events was so completely out of my control that I had no choice but to surrender at an even deeper level. It seemed like life was finally unfolding in a way that would assure the demise of whatever was left of my personal self—just what I had asked it to do so many years ago.

No one knew what was going to happen next. The trial date would almost certainly have to be reset, but no one had any idea of a new date or who the judge would be. All we could do was continue to make sure we were ready, just in case. The chief district judge, Judge Norton, took charge of finding a federal judge who could handle a four-month-long trial on short notice. In the meantime, Judge Blatt continued to hold pretrial hearings, and we continued to do very well with our motions *in limine*. Finally, unable to find a replacement judge, Judge Norton decided to take the case himself. At a hearing in July, we were given the new trial date of January 18, 2010, which was five months away. So now the chief U.S. district judge of South Carolina was going to hear the case. Everything just kept getting bigger and bigger.[4]

Judge Norton took over the pretrial hearings around August 2009. By then Randy was fully back in the saddle, and he found Judge Norton to be very bright, knowledgeable, and impartial. It turned out that Judge Norton's rulings were very similar to Judge Blatt's. We continued to tear down the government's case in pretrial motions throughout the months leading up to trial. It certainly appeared that the new judge, like the old, saw the weakness of the case being brought against us.

By October, we were three months from trial, and the time had come to reserve housing in Charleston. Years earlier I had asked Randy what the probability was of the government catching on that I didn't do anything wrong and just dropping the charges. He told me that he expected the government to drop charges against everyone except me, John Kang, and John Sessions—the CEO, the president, and the chief operations officer. Randy would have included the chief financial officer, but he had previously died of cancer.

I wanted to be sure of my odds, so I pushed Randy by asking if it would literally take divine intervention for me to avoid a trial and just walk free. He pondered for a moment and said, "Yes, it would take an act of divine intervention." With that in mind, Donna and I headed to Charleston to rent a place to live for four months. We made it an adventure. We had both lived at the Temple for more than thirty-five years. We had never been away for much more than a few weeks at a time. This trial is what it would take to force us to relocate for such an extended period. There was, of course, the possibility that my departure would be much longer.

As we approached the trial date, things unfolded in accordance to Randy's predictions. The government called in the second tier of

---

4 It is worth noting that years earlier the federal prosecutor in South Carolina who originally filed the charges had resigned, and the Department of Justice in Washington had pretty much taken over the case.

indicted executives one by one and tried to get something useful before dropping charges. Of course, there was nothing to get, and we were all glad to see our colleagues taken out of harm's way. That left the three senior executives headed for trial on January 18, 2010.

I received a call from Randy mid-December. He had gotten an indication through back channels that suddenly the government was interested in discussing a settlement. After checking it out, Randy said it seemed prosecutors had had enough, and they wanted me out of the case. We were feeling pretty confident about my position given the successes we had in the pretrial hearings. I told Randy that I wanted the charges dropped with nothing on my record. If they wanted a statement of facts, I would state that I had always believed that everything was being done in accordance with standard accounting principles, but I now saw that Bobby had been doing some things improperly. In other words, I would tell the truth and nothing else.

Somehow, just four weeks before trial, and six years since the raid, light was dispelling darkness. The government insisted that I voluntarily give up a portion of a twelve-year-old stock sale, just in case the share price had been affected by Bobby's accounting inaccuracies. I doubted that the share price would have been affected, but if it had been, that was money I didn't want or need. Then, as suddenly as the whole nightmare had begun—it was over. The government agreed to drop all charges against me.

I didn't feel joy, and I didn't feel relief. What I felt was a deep sense of appreciation that in the end, truth triumphed. It may have taken divine intervention, but the truth won. Tempering this feeling, however, was the fact that John Kang and John Sessions were still headed for trial. I had been exposed to all the documents in the case, and the only things I ever saw being done willfully wrong were the actions of Bobby Davids and his group. I knew that John Kang and John Sessions had both just done their jobs to the best of their ability. I worked with Randy so that he and his team could do all they could to provide support during the trial. They couldn't participate directly, but they were present and wrote up most of the summaries, motions, and other documents needed during and after the proceedings.

The trial went extremely well. John Kang's attorney turned out to be an excellent litigator, and he pretty much handled all the cross-examination of the government witnesses, including Bobby and his paramour from the accounting department, Caroline. By the time the government rested its case, the defense attorneys felt that almost every government witness had been turned into a favorable witness for the defense. That being the case, the defense also rested. Given what had taken place in that courtroom over the past month and a half, no one could possibly feel that the government had proven its case beyond a reasonable doubt. With both sides having rested, the case went to the jury.

The jurors did not deliberate very long. After only five or six hours, they announced that they had reached a unanimous verdict. Given what had transpired during the trial, that seemed like a reasonable amount of deliberation. On March 1, 2010, the jury gathered back in the courtroom and read the verdict: guilty as charged.

The defense was stunned. The judge dropped his head into his hands. What had happened? Post-trial interviews with the jurors showed that the case was pretty much over after opening arguments. The government had presented such a simplistic, overwhelming view of what had been done wrong in the company that most jurors had made their minds up right then. Just hearing the government tell its story had been enough for most of the jurors. It was very sad. Our legal system had not worked. The truth had not been uncovered, and John Kang and John Sessions awaited sentencing.

Only one glimmer of hope was still burning. The defense had filed a motion for dismissal based on the statute of limitations, and the judge had not yet ruled on that motion. On May 27, 2010, almost three months after trial, Judge Norton issued his ruling and dismissed the entire case against John Kang and John Sessions. In that ruling, the judge took the opportunity to again and again chastise the government for what had happened in this case. Among his other complaints, he questioned why the government would keep so many people under indictment for five years and then drop all charges just before trial. Judge Norton pointed out that this had helped drive the pretrial defense cost of the case to more than $190 million.

I was pleased that John Kang and John Sessions were free with nothing on their records. I was also encouraged that at least someone had noticed the absurdity of what had taken place. But it wasn't necessarily over: the government had the right to appeal the judge's dismissal. In case that happened, the defense had filed a motion for retrial. This motion was based on the bold argument that the jury had been mistaken—the weight of the evidence presented at trial did not support the verdict. On January 19, 2011, almost a year after trial, the whole truth and nothing but the truth finally broke through. On that day, when Judge Norton signed his ruling regarding the retrial motion, Jefferson, Mason, and Madison must have breathed a sigh of relief. After two hundred years of interpretations of what they had intended—the system had worked. Truth and Justice would have the final word after all.

It had been more than seven years since Bobby Davids had walked into the U.S. Attorney's Office in Charleston and begun telling his lies. That web of illusion gained momentum and ensnarled everything in its way. But it did not make it past the chief U.S. judge of South Carolina. Judge Norton had sat through the entire trial and heard all the evidence. The jury may have been willing to accept the government's story at face value—without holding prosecutors to a reasonable burden of proof—but the judge was not. In case his dismissal order was overruled, Judge Norton not only approved the defendants' motion for a new trial, but in a nineteen-page opinion he tore the government's case to shreds. He stated that the government had not proven that there was any conspiracy among the executives, but to the contrary, the evidence supported that the executives at Medical Manager believed that the accounting was being done properly. He went on to state that he found the government's chief witnesses, Bobby and Caroline, to be noncredible, and that Caroline appeared to just be parroting Bobby's words.

I read Judge Norton's ruling with a sense of awe and relief. Now it was over. In the end, the person who mattered most had seen through the noise and recognized the truth. I didn't know that a judge could put aside the jury's verdict because he believed it was not supported by the weight of the evidence. Judge Norton made it clear that he not only had the right to put aside the verdict, he had the obligation. This was the Constitution in its finest hour. It was framed to protect the citizens from their government. But, alas, it is just a piece of paper. The judge is the only agent through which that protection can come to life. In my eyes, both of the judges in this case are heroes. They showed why our separate branches of government create important checks and balances against one another. These judges had taken a vow to protect the Constitution, and they selflessly did just that.[5]

---

5 For those interested, the government chose not to appeal Judge Norton's dismissal of the case. In the end, all the indicted Medical Manager executives walked away free.

56

Returning to the Beginning

When the smoke cleared, the whirlwind of life had dropped me off exactly where she had picked me up. After forty years, I still lived just down the field from the house I had built when I moved to the woods to meditate. I was still meeting with people every morning and evening for services in the Temple, including the large Sunday morning gatherings started back in 1972. But the original ten acres the Temple sat on was now surrounded by nine hundred acres of rolling fields and beautiful forests over which life had made us steward. The foundations of my life had remained completely undisturbed throughout this entire dance with the Universal Flow.

The legal ordeal quickly became a distant memory, almost a dream. It had come and gone, just like everything else. I could clearly see that because I had inwardly surrendered each step of the way, no scars were left on my psyche. It had been like writing on water—the impressions only lasted while the events were actually taking place. Yet in the moment of actual experience, each twist and turn had reached deep inside me and forced me past foundational fears and personal boundaries. As long as I was willing to accept the purification power of life's flow, I kept coming out on the other side a transformed person. How could I consider this a bad experience when it created such beauty and freedom within me? To the contrary, I stand in awe of all that has happened since I started this amazing experiment of acceptance and surrender.

One thing is for certain: he who left on this journey—never

returned. The flow of life had served as sandpaper that, to a great extent, freed me of myself. Unable to unbind myself from the incessant pull of my psyche, in an act of sheer desperation, I had thrown myself into the arms of life. From that point forward, all I did was my very best to serve what was put in front of me and let go of what it stirred up within me. Joy and pain, success and failure, praise and blame—they all had pulled at what was so deeply rooted within me. The more I let go, the freer I became. It was not my responsibility to find what was binding me; that was life's job. My responsibility was to willingly let go of whatever was brought up within me.

After seeing all I'd seen over the years, surrender to the flow of life was all that was left of me. No longer busy making other plans, I settled into the quiet life of increased solitude in which I once again found myself. It soon became obvious that life had provided me the ideal environment in which to write this book. The moment I sat down, the inspiration flowed in like a tidal wave. I began writing what I always knew I would have to write—what happened when I let go.

People often ask me how I look at things now that I've gone through the life-changing experiences of these past forty years. I tell them to read *The Untethered Soul*. How could I possibly explain the great freedom that comes from realizing to the depth of your being that life knows what it's doing? Only direct experience can take you there. At some point there's no more struggle, just the deep peace that comes from surrendering to a perfection that is beyond your comprehension. Eventually, even the mind stops resisting, and the heart loses the tendency to close. The joy, excitement, and freedom are simply too beautiful to give up. Once you are ready to let go of yourself, life becomes your friend, your teacher, your secret lover. When life's way becomes your way, all the noise stops, and there is a great peace.

In eternal gratitude for all the experiences we call Life . . .

MAS, March 2015

ABOUT THE AUTHOR

MICHAEL A. SINGER is the author of the #1 *New York Times* bestseller *The Untethered Soul.* He had a deep inner awakening in 1971 while working on his doctorate in economics and went into seclusion to focus on yoga and meditation. In 1975, he founded Temple of the Universe, a now long-established yoga and meditation center where people of any religion or set of beliefs can come together to experience inner peace. He is also the creator of a leading-edge software package that transformed the medical practice management industry, and founding CEO of a billion-dollar public company whose achievements are archived in the Smithsonian Institution. Along with his more than four decades of spiritual teaching, Michael has made major contributions in the areas of business, education, health care, and environmental protection.

MORE BY THE AUTHOR

Audio Lectures: A number of Michael A. Singer's talks on spiritual growth are available in audio format. Visit www.untetheredsoul.com for more information.

Books: In addition to *The Untethered Soul,* Michael A. Singer has previously authored two books on the integration of Eastern and Western philosophy: *The Search for Truth* and *Three Essays on Universal Law: Karma, Will, and Love.* Available on www.amazon.com.

Music: *Songs of the Untethered Soul.* Eight inspiring songs, written by Michael A. Singer and sung by musician Kathy Zavada, meant to still the mind and open the heart. Visit www.songsoftheuntetheredsoul.com

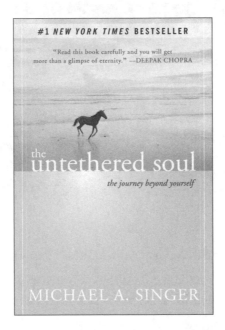

Enjoy a FREE video series and continue your journey with Michael A. Singer

Join Michael in this three-part "mini-course" exploring:

- Why We Suffer—Michael describes the struggle to "fix inner problems using the outside world" and the consequences of an out-of-control mind.

- Your Beautiful Mind—Michael reveals the deeper, intuitive and creative levels of the mind that are universally accessible.

- Learning to Let Go—Discover a transformational inner process of "spiritual purification" where we release unconscious patterns in order to restore the natural flow of our life energy.

Sign Up for This FREE Video Series
by Michael A. Singer
www.SurrenderCourse.com